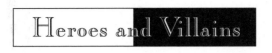

OSKAR SCHINDLER

Other books in the Heroes and Villains series include:
Al Capone
Frederick Douglass
Adolf Hitler
King Arthur

Heroes and Villains

OSKAR SCHINDLER

John F. Wukovits

LUCENT
BOOKS ®

THOMSON

GALE

San Diego • Detroit • New York • San Francisco • Cleveland • New Haven, Conn. • Waterville, Maine • London • Munich

LIBRARY OF CONGRESS CATALOGING-IN-PUBLICATION DATA

Wukovits, John F., 1944–
    Oskar Schindler / John F. Wukovits.
        p. cm. — (Heroes and Villains)
    Includes bibliographical references and index.
Summary : A biography of the profit-hungry businessman who became a protector
and savior of the Jews during the Nazi holocaust.
    ISBN 1-56006-952-X (alk. paper)
    1.Schindler, Oskar, 1908–1974.—Juvenile literature. 2 Righteous Gentiles in
the Holocaust—Biography—Juvenile literature. 3. Holocaust, Jewish (1939–1945)—
Juvenile literature. 4. World War, 1939–1945. 5. Jews—Persecution—Poland—
Juvenile literature. 6. Jews—Persecutions—Czech Republic—Juvenile literature. [1.
Schindler, Oskar, 1908–1974. 2. Righteous Gentiles in the Holocaust. 3. World War,
1939–1945—Jews—Rescue. 4. Holocaust, Jewish (1939–1945)] I. Title. II. Heroes and
villains series
    D804.66.S38 W85 2003
    362.87'81'092—dc21

2002002221

Printed in the United States of America

Contents

Good and evil are an ever-present feature of human history. Their presence is reflected through the ages in tales of great heroism and extraordinary villainy. Such tales provide insight into human nature, whether they involve two people or two thousand, for the essence of heroism and villainy is found in deeds rather than in numbers. It is the deeds that pique our interest and lead us to wonder what prompts a man or woman to perform such acts.

Samuel Johnson, the eminent eighteenth-century English writer, once wrote, "The two great movers of the human mind are the desire for good, and fear of evil." The pairing of desire and fear, possibly two of the strongest human emotions, helps explain the intense fascination people have with all things good and evil—and by extension, heroic and villainous.

People are attracted to the person who reaches into a raging river to pull a child from what could have been a watery grave for both, and to the person who risks his or her own life to shepherd hundreds of desperate black slaves to safety on the Underground Railroad. We wonder what qualities these heroes possess that enable them to act against self-interest, and even their own survival. We also wonder if, under similar circumstances, we would behave as they do.

Evil, on the other hand, horrifies as well as intrigues us. Few people can look upon the drifter who mutilates and kills a neighbor or the dictator who presides over the torture and murder of thousands of his own citizens without feeling a sense of revulsion. And yet, as Joseph Conrad writes, we experience "the fascination of the abomination." How else to explain the overwhelming success of a book such as Truman Capote's *In Cold Blood*, which examines in horrifying detail a vicious and senseless murder that took place in the American heartland in the 1960s? The popularity of murder mysteries and Court TV are also evidence of the human fascination with villainy.

Most people recoil in the face of such evil. Yet most feel a deep-seated curiosity about the kind of person who could commit a terrible act. It is perhaps a reflection of our innermost fears that we wonder whether we could resist or stand up to such behavior in our presence or even if we ourselves possess the capacity to commit such terrible crimes.

The Lucent Books Heroes and Villains series capitalizes on our fascination with the perpetrators of both good and evil by introducing readers to some of history's most revered heroes and hated villains. These include heroes such as Frederick Douglass, who knew firsthand the humiliation of slavery and, at great risk to himself, publicly fought to abolish the institution of slavery in America. It also includes villains such as Adolf Hitler, who is remembered both for the devastation of Europe and for the murder of 6 million Jews and thousands of Gypsies, Slavs, and others whom Hitler deemed unworthy of life.

Each book in the Heroes and Villains series examines the life story of a hero or villain from history. Generous use of primary and secondary source quotations gives readers eyewitness views of the life and times of each individual as well as enlivens the narrative. Notes and annotated bibliographies provide stepping-stones to further research.

"We Only Did What We Had To"

The years immediately preceding and during World War II produced much greater misery than that typically seen in wartime. Besides the usual appalling list of deaths and injuries caused by the fighting, that era gave birth to the Holocaust, an unimaginable period of bigotry and hatred that caused the deaths of millions of people. It made decent people everywhere wonder whether humankind had, indeed, improved from the barbarism that had more commonly been associated with ages past. Men, women, and children met hideous deaths or torture, not because of any crime they had committed but simply because of their race and religious beliefs.

Most of this intolerance came at the hands of the Nazi Party, founded and led by German leader Adolf Hitler,

and much of its animosity was directed toward Europe's Jewish population. The perpetrators of the Holocaust forced Jewish children out of schools, shut down Jewish-owned businesses, drove entire families from their homes, herded millions into concentration camps, and transformed murder into such a ruthlessly efficient, mass-produced phenomenon that today the word *Nazi* is synonymous with evil.

Out of the Holocaust, however, a few individuals rose up to assert that, although indecency may have dominated the times, it would be a short-lived aberration that would one day disappear into the recesses of the past. Some gave their lives to oppose Hitler and his Nazis; others sheltered Jews from danger and deportation by providing hiding places. In the long run, these individuals prevailed and helped free the world from the grips of Nazism.

A Wartime Fortune

Oskar Schindler was one such person. Born in Czechoslovakia, he loved money, good food, alcohol, fast cars, and women. To support his extravagant lifestyle, Schindler opened a lucrative factory that produced mess kits and utensils for the German army. His factory became so profitable that from 1939 to 1944, Schindler joined the select rank of multimillionaire.

Two factors helped Schindler gain his enormous income. In the 1930s Schindler joined the Nazi Party, not because he agreed with Hitler's hateful views or political stance—Schindler had few, if any, prejudices—but because members of the Nazi Party immediately gained the inside track on contracts with the German military. Membership in the Nazi Party gave a person access to high government and military officials, and the affable Schindler made the most of these associations. As contracts poured into his offices in Krakow, Poland, Schindler became one of the

Nazi dictator Adolf Hitler salutes his troops, flanked by SS leader Heinrich Himmler. Hitler's brutal Nazi regime murdered millions of people during World War II.

Laws Against the Jews

A stream of anti-Semitic laws suffocated the Jews under Hitler's control. Edicts governed every part of their lives, from education to romance, and business to home. The following are just a few of the many laws imposed on Jews during the Holocaust.

- Jews could not attend regular schools.
- Jews had to carry identification cards.
- Jews could not attend movies or concerts.
- Jews could not own or drive cars.
- Jews could not attend universities.
- Jews could not own telephones.
- Jews could sit only on park benches clearly labeled for Jews.

wealthiest men in Nazi-dominated territory.

A more sinister factor also helped Schindler become wealthy: He built his success on the backs of Jewish slave labor. Instead of paying the standard wages to area laborers, like most of his fellow businessmen, Schindler used Jewish inmates from a nearby concentration camp. He still had to pay money to Nazi authorities for these workers, but the amount fell far short of the expenses he would have incurred had he hired non-Jewish men and women. However, Schindler never abused his Jewish labor force; he never beat, whipped, or punished them. In fact, he made sure that they were well treated and received more food than normally allotted by the Nazis to

Jewish inmates. He employed them in his factory simply because it was good business—the less he paid for workers, the more he reaped for himself.

The Puzzle That Is Oskar Schindler

Then Schindler changed. Instead of worrying about schedules and contracts, he fretted over the safety of Jewish fathers, mothers, sons, and daughters. A man who had never before shown much concern for the welfare of anyone but himself suddenly took on a new role. And as the war came to a close in 1945, Schindler spent his vast fortune to save his Jewish workers from death.

Why he changed has remained something of an enigma to this day.

One can speculate by examining his actions and studying his words, but no one—even the Jews he saved—can adequately explain the motivations behind the complex Oskar Schindler. There certainly was no financial reason for what he did; he freely spent his money to help others. Yet Schindler transformed from a profit-hungry businessman to protector and savior.

The people he sheltered care little about Schindler's motivation. Some claim that he loved being a father figure to so many individuals. Others say that sheltering so many Jews filled a void in Schindler's own life, giving him a sense of family that he lacked as a child and as a married man. A few even argue that Schindler helped his workers because it still made good business sense. Most of Schindler's Jews, however, do not worry about motives. They are simply grateful that he did what he did and freely testify

Oskar Schindler receives a hero's welcome during a visit to Israel in 1962 from some of the more than eleven hundred Holocaust survivors he saved.

Pastor Niemöller

One of the most famous opponents of Adolf Hitler was the German Protestant minister Pastor Martin Niemöller. At a time when many of his fellow clergy, both Protestant and Catholic, remained silent, Niemöller spoke out against the tyranny imposed by Hitler. He urged people to take a stand, and contributed one of the most powerful statements advocating the need for action when he uttered the following words (taken from Michael Berenbaum's history of the Holocaust, The World Must Know*).*

First they came for the socialists, and I did not speak out—because I was not a socialist.

Then they came for the trade unionists, and I did not speak out—because I was not a trade unionist.

Then they came for the Jews, and I did not speak out—because I was not a Jew.

Then they came for me—and there was no one left to speak for me.

Pastor Martin Niemöller dared to speak out against Nazi atrocities at a time when many of his fellow clergy remained silent.

Schindler (second from left) poses in 1940 with some of the factory employees that would likely have perished during the Holocaust without his assistance.

that they survived the war only because of Schindler.

Was Oskar Schindler heroic? According to his wife, Emilie, "Steven Spielberg's film, Thomas Keneally's book, and all the rivers of ink spilled fifty years after the facts depict my husband as a hero for this century. This is not true. He was not a hero, and neither was I. We only did what we had to."[1]

Part of Emilie's statement results from humility, part from honesty. Often, men and women who have taken action during extraordinary events claim that they did nothing heroic, that they only did what anyone else would do under similar circumstances.

Emilie Schindler and the others who mutter those sentiments are wrong. A hero is not only the individual who charges straight into enemy gunfire or rushes into a burning building to save a life. A hero is someone who does what he or she must do despite the difficulties. Some people shrink from doing what they must. Heroes do not. Oskar Schindler was one such person.

Chapter One

Acting to the Circumstances

For a man whose name is recognized worldwide because of Steven Spielberg's powerful movie *Schindler's List*, Oskar Schindler's early life rests in relative obscurity. Not much has been uncovered by researchers, but what little is known reveals a few of the influences that shaped this man. Those influences combined to mold an individual replete with contradictions: a man who hated school yet became successful, who loved his mother yet grew distant from his father, who remained married to the same woman for forty-six years yet flagrantly ignored her for other women, and an individual who loved money and luxuries yet surrendered them to help others. Most important, Oskar Schindler was a man who lacked interest in intellectual pursuits but

who, in the end, taught the world a lesson not to be forgotten.

An Early Influence

Oskar Schindler was born on April 28, 1908, in Zwittau, a small industrial town nestled in the coal region of the Jesenik Mountains in Czechoslovakia. Zwittau, in part of Czechoslovakia called the Sudetenland, stood only a few miles from the German border and contained a large German-speaking population, including the Schindlers. Oskar's father Hans, who owned a farm machinery plant, had been born in a region controlled by Austria that enjoyed close ties with Germany. Hans identified with that nation and typically spoke German at dinner or during business.

Most nights, Hans could be found at the local coffeehouses engaged in heated debates about current events, smoking cigars, and sipping on the cognac he so loved. Although the fun-loving Hans provided a comfortable home with its own gardens for his family—wife Louisa, Oskar, and daughter Elfriede— he ignored his wife. The marriage dissolved into a union without passion and romance. In the absence of a loving companion, Oskar's mother turned to religion for comfort. A devout Catholic, Louisa spent as much time at church as Hans did at the coffeehouses.

As a result, Oskar and younger sister Elfriede enjoyed the necessities of life yet lacked the nurturing devotion and security that come from a well-adjusted, happy family. Whenever Oskar incurred his father's wrath, which occurred frequently, he ran to the neighboring home of his two childhood friends, the Kantor boys, to seek advice and acceptance from their father. Dr. Felix Kantor, a rabbi in the Zwittau Jewish community, dispensed comforting words on a regular basis to young Oskar. Because of their relationship, Oskar never developed a hatred for Jews that afflicted so many of his Christian neighbors. He knew the

Schindler grew up in a small Czechoslovakian town in the Sudetenland, a mountainous area that bordered Germany, where many ethnic Germans lived.

Kantors were friendly, helpful, and caring, regardless of their religion.

Love of Women, Speed, and Danger

Since Zwittau had such a large German-speaking population, Schindler attended German schools, where he took classes in engineering and business in preparation to take over his father's factory. However, books and study bored the young Schindler, who preferred spending his time playing sports or in the company of female classmates. And girls loved the dashing youth. Schindler impressed them with his suave manner and tenderness.

Schindler's other passion revolved around machines, especially those that he could race. Schindler loved speed and exquisitely designed motorcycles almost as much as the attention racing brought him and its inherent sense of danger. He built his own motorcycle, which he entered in area competitions. Then, during his senior year in high school, Schindler stepped up to European races after his father bought him a powerful red Galloni motorcycle, an expensive vehicle that few Czechs owned.

Schindler poses at the wheel of his car with his father, Hans, in 1929. The young Schindler loved racing and women.

In the spring of 1928 the twenty-year-old Schindler joined the elite group of motorcycle racers when his father bought a Moto-Guzzi motorcycle, then considered the finest and most expensive vehicle of its type. Only four other European racers owned a Moto-Guzzi, and all were professionals competing on the European circuit. Schindler joined them in a 1928 mountain race, in which he finished a surprising third. In his second race, he led for much of the way until dropping to fourth in the final stretch.

Life with Emilie

Schindler moved just as fast in matters of the heart. That same year he met Emilie Pelze, who came from the nearby village of Alt-Molstein. Dignified, shy, and educated in a convent by Catholic nuns, Emilie appeared to be the opposite of Schindler. According to Emilie, who was born six months before Schindler, the two met when Oskar and his father appeared at her farm to sell an electrical motor to her father. While Hans Schindler embarked on a lengthy sales pitch, Oskar kept sneaking looks at Emilie. She remembers, "He seemed bored with what his father was saying, a long spiel about technology, electricity, and progress. He soon tried to engage my complicity by means of suggestive glances and half smiles."[2]

At first, Emilie rejected Oskar's suggestions that they date, but the persistent Schindler refused to be spurned. He often returned to the Pelze farm, each time claiming he was there only to sell a motor. Really he came with the intent of winning Emilie. She quickly gave in, and within a month Oskar asked for her hand in marriage. "I want to unite my life to Emilie's," he told her parents, "so that we can build a future together."[3]

Local residents were skeptical of Schindler's whirlwind courtship of Emilie. Many claimed he was only interested in her wealthy father's money. Others doubted that the young man could remain faithful to one woman.

Despite people's worries, Oskar and Emilie married on March 6, 1928, only six weeks after first meeting. The handsome Schindler and his shy bride made such an impression on Emilie's grandmother that on the wedding day she kept telling people that Emilie looked like Sleeping Beauty just awakened by Oskar, the charming prince who had come to save her. According to Emilie, the prince received a dowry, or wedding gift, of one hundred thousand Czech crowns from her father, a substantial sum of money at the time.

The couple moved in with Oskar's family in Zwittau, occupying the second floor. Emilie found the hot-tempered Hans Schindler difficult, though. A few months later, the two moved into a large house in Moravia, a Czech province near Zwittau, that once belonged to a wealthy family.

Anti-Semitism

Anti-Semitism, which is the discrimination and hatred of the Jews, has persisted for thousands of years. Much of the bitter feelings have been inflamed by statements made by Christian leaders who were angered that the Jews did not consider Jesus Christ the son of God and who contended that Jews were the killers of Christ. Historian Daniel Jonah Goldhagen, in his 1996 book *Hitler's Willing Executioners,* includes the following quote from one of the Catholic Church's foremost leaders of the fourth century, Father John Chrysostom: "Where Christ-killers gather, the cross is ridiculed, God blasphemed, the father unacknowledged, the son insulted, the grace of the Spirit rejected. If the Jewish rites are holy and venerable, our way of life must be false. But if our way is true, as indeed it is, theirs is fraudulent."

Harsh sentiments were not confined to Catholic theologians, however. As recorded by Gay Block and Malka Drucker in their 1992 book, *Rescuers: Portraits of Moral Courage in the Holocaust,* German religious leader Martin Luther stated in 1543, "Know, Christians, that next to the devil thou hast no enemy more cruel, more venomous and violent than a true Jew. Their synagogues should be set on fire, and whatever does not burn up should be covered or spread over with dirt so that no one may ever be able to see a cinder or stone of it."

In Moravia, the newlyweds found peace for a time. However, in the early 1930s Schindler left to serve in the Czech army, which was a requirement for every male resident. He hated the confining military lifestyle, and as soon as his term ended he rushed back to Moravia.

Unfortunately for Emilie, she was not the primary reason he wanted to return. The fun-loving Schindler began to ignore his wife. He filled his days with his sales work and his nights with frivolity. Schindler engaged in a seemingly endless stream of women, parties, and alcohol. He developed a passion for cognac, frequently lacing his coffee with generous helpings. Emilie, meanwhile, had to be content with solitary pastimes in an empty home.

With his trademark double-breasted suits, Panama hats, and hearty laughs, Schindler made friends wherever he went. He also had an amazing ability to persuade people to see things his way or to conclude that he was, after all, a noble fellow. He could seemingly sell electrical appliances to anybody. A few wary individuals, however, doubted his sincerity and began calling him "Swindler."

Schindler impressed adoring females by sending as many as one hundred roses as thanks for an evening's entertainment. He also wore so much cologne that people often smelled him before they saw him. While Emilie remained at home, Schindler developed short relationships with numerous women. He fathered illegitimate twins in the 1930s and another child during the war.

His many affairs did not go unnoticed by Emilie. Even though she argued with her husband about his unfaithfulness, she never threatened to leave him, claiming in part that a divorce would devastate her Catholic parents. More important though, was the spell that Oskar seemed to hold over Emilie. No matter how many girls occupied her husband's time, she never fell out of love with him. One night, for instance, after the two ended another heated argument over Schindler's indiscretions, Emilie was the one who slept on the couch outside the bedroom while Oskar enjoyed the warmth of their much-larger bed. He simply possessed too much charisma and appeal for his wife to stay angry.

"In spite of his flaws, Oskar had a big heart and was always ready to help whoever was in need," Emilie later wrote. "He was affable, kind, extremely generous and charitable, but at the same time, not mature at all. He constantly lied and deceived me, and later returned feeling sorry, like a boy caught in mischief, asking to be forgiven one more time. And then we would start all over again."[4]

1935: A Pivotal Year

The year 1935 was not a good one for Schindler. Relations with his father, Hans, deteriorated when his father abandoned his mother. Oskar refused to talk with Hans about the issue. Later that year, two additional blows to family stability happened in speedy succession: Hans's farm machinery business went bankrupt, and Schindler's mother suddenly died. In a brief span, Schindler lost everything that was important to him—both parents, one through death and the other through marital discord, and the family business. On top of that, Schindler himself did not enjoy a happy marriage.

After his father's business dissolved, Schindler accepted a position as a sales manager for an electrical machinery firm, Moravian Electrotechnic. It was a job that required Schindler to be on the road much of the time. With his powers of persuasion, Schindler proved successful in the field, but the change did little to help a deteriorating situation at home.

Nevertheless, Schindler soon saw an opportunity to make a profit in the developing political situation. He and Emilie lived in the Sudetenland, an area once governed by Germany and still containing large numbers of German-speaking people. When Adolf Hitler

Konrad Henlein inspects Sudeten German Party corps. Henlein's organization espoused Hitler's racist beliefs and called for German annexation of the Sudetenland.

rose to power in 1933, many Sudeten Czechs joined Konrad Henlein's Sudeten German Party, an organization that urged a return to Germany and an adherence to Hitler's beliefs.

One of those beliefs stated that Jews should not be welcomed in German society. Dating back thousands of years in Europe and the Middle East, Jews had felt the sting of prejudice at the hands of Christian and Arab neighbors. Catholic and Protestant leaders alike stirred the pas-

sions of hatred by denouncing Jews as evil and as being responsible for the death of Jesus Christ. The inflammatory remarks produced outbursts of violence against the Jewish community, and Hitler's audacious program was only the latest in a long list of such events.

In 1935 Schindler joined the Henlein party. Although he understood the party's beliefs toward Jews, he did so out of purely economic reasons. He held no bitterness toward the Jews; his association with the Kantor family in his youth precluded that. Instead, Schindler saw his membership as a way of increasing business sales—the more associations with community leaders he could form, the more contracts he could sell. As Emilie explained, "Oskar was not a man of political principles: he just acted according to the circumstances."[5]

First Associations with the Nazis

Three years later, Adolf Hitler annexed the Sudetenland after threatening a war if Czechoslovakia did not return the land to German control. The Nazi Party absorbed Henlein's association, and again, realizing that he could make money out of a political situation, Schindler joined the Nazi Party. The harsh actions by Nazis against Czech citizens and property, especially those directed toward Jews, upset Schindler, but he shoved the unpleasant thoughts to the back of his mind so that he could concentrate on accumulating wealth.

That same year, Schindler's love of excitement and danger compelled him to plunge even deeper into the world of Nazism. He served as a spy for the Abwehr, the Nazi intelligence-gathering organization. One of his mistresses,

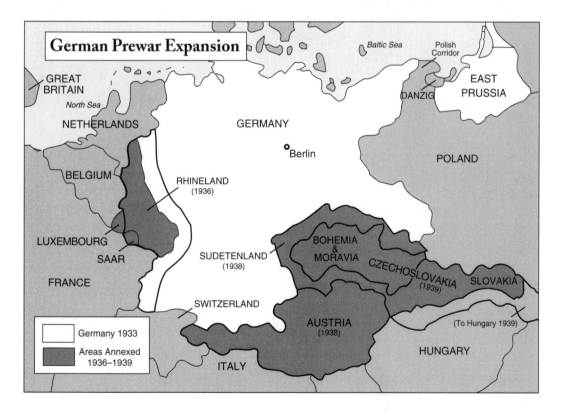

German Prewar Expansion

GREAT BRITAIN

North Sea

NETHERLANDS

GERMANY

Berlin

Baltic Sea

Polish Corridor

DANZIG

EAST PRUSSIA

POLAND

BELGIUM

RHINELAND (1936)

LUXEMBOURG

SAAR

FRANCE

SUDETENLAND (1938)

SWITZERLAND

BOHEMIA & MORAVIA

CZECHOSLOVAKIA (1939)

SLOVAKIA

AUSTRIA (1938)

(To Hungary 1939)

HUNGARY

ITALY

Germany 1933

Areas Annexed 1936–1939

Eva Scheuer, introduced Schindler to a German Abwehr agent named Eberhard Gebauer. Gebauer knew that Schindler's business frequently took him to nearby Poland, so he offered Schindler a job collecting information about the Polish army.

Schindler, sensing another chance to make money, readily accepted, and soon he was off to Poland. In fact, one of his actions played a role in the opening act of World War II. Schindler bribed a Polish soldier to steal Polish uniforms, which he forwarded to the Abwehr. The German army made copies of these uniforms. Later, they were worn by German soldiers in a September 1939 "raid" against German troops. The "raid" was made to look like it was carried out by Polish soldiers, but the invaders were actually German troops dressed in the stolen and copied Polish uniforms. The Germans yelled orders in Polish, and even dressed the dead bodies of concentration camp inmates in Polish uniforms so it appeared an attack on Germany had taken place. Hitler used this fabricated action as justification for his invasion into Poland. Within

Hitler leads a victory parade through a Czechoslovakian city after the Sudetenland was ceded to the Nazis in 1938.

The Sudetenland

The reasons why Adolf Hitler wanted Germany to regain control of the Sudetenland stem from World War I (1914–1918). When Germany lost that war, the nation had to yield control of the Sudetenland to the newly formed nation of Czechoslovakia. For twenty years, the transfer of land containing so many German-speaking inhabitants irritated German politicians. In 1938 Hitler, backed by a potent German military machine, demanded the land's return. To avoid war, at a September 29–30, 1938, meeting, the British prime minister, Neville Chamberlain, Premier Edouard Daladier of France, and Italy's Benito Mussolini forced the Czechoslovakian government to yield and signed the Munich Pact, which agreed to return the Sudetenland to Germany.

days, much of Europe was involved in the war.

Before war erupted, a spy for the Czech government located incriminating papers in Schindler's bedroom, which led to his being arrested for his activities with the Abwehr. Czech authorities sentenced Schindler to death, but fortunately for him, he was released when Adolf Hitler annexed the Sudetenland in late September 1938.

Within a year, Schindler followed the German army into Poland, intent on building an economic empire in the newly controlled land. The man who came from a family that proudly boasted a close association with German culture had shifted from racing cars and selling electrical machinery to conducting business with the German military. His move led to associations with top-ranking Nazi officials and a profitable industry.

Chapter Two

"I'm Gonna Make a Lot of Money"

The German military stunned the world on September 1, 1939, when it invaded Poland. Within days, Great Britain and France entered the war against Hitler, setting the stage for five years of slaughter. Before September faded, Poland capitulated and fell under the harsh rule of Nazism. While world events raced toward their deadly conclusions, one individual moved quickly to take advantage of the situation. One week after German soldiers poured across the Polish border, Oskar Schindler arrived in one of the nation's largest cities, Krakow, to establish a new business. His work would bring him in close contact with Nazi officials and would place him in many perilous situations.

Budding Friendship with Itzhak Stern

Wartime often brings out the best and the worst of intentions in people. While many of his fellow countrymen answered the call of duty and served in the military, Schindler saw the war as a golden opportunity to profit. He figured that if he could establish an industry that supplied essential goods to the German army, he could avoid serving in the military while also amassing a huge fortune. Hitler's actions toward the Jews did not concern Schindler. Money did. As historian Elinor J. Brecher explained, "He didn't go into World War II thinking, 'I'm gonna save Jews and be a hero.' He went into it thinking, 'I'm gonna make a lot of money and be set for life.'"[6]

Krakow stood within an hour's traveling time from the Czech border. Schindler realized that with the ties he had established during his work for the Abwehr, plus the contacts he made as a member of the Nazi Party, he would probably receive little formal opposition to his plan to open a factory. All he had to do was locate suitable buildings and determine which products to manufacture. Itzhak Stern helped him do both.

A Jewish bookkeeper in Krakow since 1924, Stern knew as much about Krakow's industrial community as anyone. One day in early September, Stern's boss introduced an impeccably dressed Schindler to Stern, mentioned that Schindler sought a business opportunity, and asked Stern to share his knowledge with the foreigner. The friendly Schindler thrust out his hand in greeting, but Stern did not. When Schindler asked why, Stern explained that it broke the law for a Jew to shake the hand of a German. Schindler turned in disgust at what he considered a silly rule.

Stern did not know what to think of this man. His mother had already disappeared into the Auschwitz concentration camp, so he was wary of any

Schindler greets Itzhak Stern in 1949. The German businessman and the Jewish bookkeeper developed a close bond while working together.

Nazi he met. "I must admit now that I was intensely suspicious of Schindler for a long time,"[7] Stern later remarked. Something, though, about Schindler made Stern respond. He sensed a compassion in Schindler that he rarely saw in Nazi officials, and over time, a close bond would develop between the two, almost a father-son relationship. Stern would become the moral compass for Schindler as the war unfolded, quietly mentioning the atrocities plaguing fellow Jews and hinting that Schindler could help.

The Good Life

Stern examined the various business opportunities in Krakow and advised Schindler on what he could purchase. Through his contacts in the German military, the astute Schindler agreed to manufacture materials that every soldier needed—mess kits and field kitchenware—thus guaranteeing him a

Dr. Hans Frank

The top Nazi in Poland, Dr. Hans Frank, started his career in the Nazi Party as a lawyer who defended Hitler and Hitler's interests before he became head of the German government. According to Norman Polmar and Thomas B. Allen's *World War II: The Encyclopedia of the War Years, 1941–1945,* as reward for his superb legal work, Hitler named Frank to the top post in Poland. There, he could expect to profit from the country's many treasures resting in large Polish farms, in cathedrals, and in government offices. Under Frank's ruthlessly efficient guidance, almost the entire Jewish population residing in Poland disappeared into one of the many concentration camps. Following the war, Frank stood trial for his crimes and was hanged on October 16, 1946.

Hans Frank served as governor-general of Nazi-occupied Poland.

The entrance to Schindler's German Enamelware Factory. Schindler's workers, who were mostly Polish Jews, nicknamed the factory Emalia.

steady market. Schindler then settled on an abandoned enamelware business that had gone into bankruptcy, arranged to receive ownership from the Court of Commercial Claims, and opened for business in December 1939. Schindler named his factory the *Deutsche Emailwaren Fabrik,* the German Enamelware Factory. German officials simply called it DEF, while Polish workers hired to work the machinery nicknamed the place Emalia.

Stern then put Schindler in contact with another influential Jewish businessman, Abraham Bankier, who helped arrange financing for Schindler's business. In exchange for a substantial amount of money from some of Krakow's Jews, who feared they would soon lose their money to the Nazis anyway and figured they may as well invest in a plan backed by their friend Stern, Schindler agreed to deliver a monthly quota of products from his factory that the Jewish businessmen could use to trade on the black market (an illegal system of selling and acquiring products not available in stores).

Much of Schindler's workforce came from Krakow's Jewish community, who chafed under the increasing German restrictions on their lives. Since by law he did not have to pay the Jews as much money as non-Jewish labor, Schindler turned a handsome profit for much of the war. By 1941 he had almost 200 Jews working for him, and the number expanded to 550 when Schindler began producing antitank shells later that year. The addition of war armaments carried the extra bonus of making Emalia an industry essential to the war effort. This resulted in Schindler's having greater authority and made it less likely that the Nazis would shut down his factory and ship off the Jewish workers.

Schindler quickly became a millionaire. The money financed his luxuriant lifestyle, which he enjoyed to its fullest. He lived in a beautiful Krakow apartment and adorned it with all sorts of porcelain vases, expensive Persian rugs, and plush curtains. That the apartment had been confiscated from its previous owners—a wealthy Jewish family—did not seem to bother Schindler. He was too busy making money and enjoying life.

While Emilie remained at their Czechoslovakian home, Schindler spent his evenings in the company of German officials and beautiful women. Money flowed through his fingers like water—he thought nothing of tipping taxi drivers twice the amount of the fare—and women found him irresistible. He established relations with a number of females, including a German woman named Ingrid and his Polish secretary, Victoria Klonowska. One woman who knew him at the

Schindler (pictured in front of Emalia) became a millionaire from his factory's profits.

time said that Oskar "was a fantastic-looking man. He had this savoir faire [charm]. There was not one woman who would not like to have him in bed."[8] While Schindler lived a life of luxury, only thirty miles away Jews perished in the death camp of Auschwitz.

Life Worsens for Krakow's Jews

As Schindler's enamelware business prospered, Jews in Poland saw their lives altered in drastic ways. Almost every day, new evidence indicated the hideous extent of Hitler's program for Poland. Under Dr. Hans Frank, the top Nazi official in Poland, Krakow's Jews

Life in the Ghetto

Shortly after the German troops entered Poland, Nazi authorities implemented a program to confine all Jews into ghettos, neighborhoods in larger cities that could be walled off from the non-Jewish portions. At a later time, the Jews would be relocated to death camps.

Jews lived in constant fear of being deported and separated from loved ones. However, Nazi authority was not to be challenged. In this quote from David A. Adler's We Remember the Holocaust, *Hirsch Altusky, a Jew who lived in a Polish ghetto, gives one example of what happened when a Jew disobeyed authority.*

A Polish police officer caught a Jew who was in some sort of trouble. The Jew injured the policeman, and that night they took all the men from Nine Nalewski Street, fifty-one men. No one knew for quite a few days what happened to them. But then the Judenrat [the Jewish governing council in the ghetto] was notified to pick up the bodies and was told to pay for the bullets the Nazis used to kill the men.

Warsaw ghetto police stop and search a man wearing an armband that identifies him as a Jew.

were to be removed and sent to one of twelve labor camps in the area. In late 1939, Frank issued laws stating that every Jewish individual had to wear a white armband with a yellow Star of David emblem on their left arm, and every male between the ages of fourteen and sixty had to register and be transported to one of the labor camps.

Dr. Frank ordered Krakow to be clear of Jews by the summer of 1941. More than forty thousand of the city's sixty thousand Jews speedily disappeared into labor camps. The remainder gathered whatever valuables they could, left their homes, and relocated to a ghetto in Krakow's southern section. Since Schindler's factory needed its workers, Nazi authorities made sure that his Jewish laborers remained in the Krakow ghetto instead of being sent away.

The move into the ghetto—a word that in those days meant a section of town where Jews were required to live—occurred in March 1941. Lugging bags of clothing and other valuable items, Jewish families shuffled by high walls that separated the ghetto from the rest of Krakow, then entered tiny apartments that would be shared with other

A Jewish family relocates to the Krakow ghetto in 1941 during the forced evacuation of the city's remaining Jews.

families. No Jew could leave the ghetto without written permission. The only Jews who could depart were those with proper identification cards denoting them as workers in a factory. Schindler's laborers received a yellow card imprinted with their photograph and a large "J." Each morning, Nazi guards marched them to Emalia, then marched them back at night.

That same month, Nazi officials declared that no Jewish worker could be paid a wage. Instead, the money would be given to Nazi headquarters in Krakow. From then on, Schindler had to pay his German superiors $2.50 each day for a skilled worker and $1.65 for an unskilled laborer. The Jews had to live strictly off the meager rations they received in the ghetto.

Schindler immediately recognized the hardship this placed on his workers. He knew they needed more food, not simply to survive but to be efficient workers in his factory. The only way they would receive extra food, however, was if he purchased food on the black market. Realizing that his factory's productivity would suffer unless his workers remained healthy, Schindler started to buy additional food.

However, other disturbing events soon diverted Schindler's attention. In the fall of 1941, without warning, Nazi troops started to seize people from the Krakow ghetto. These *Aktionen,* or organized removals of Jewish families, had one purpose—to

eventually eliminate all traces of Jews in Poland.

Rumors abounded over what happened to the Jews who disappeared. Some claimed they lived in communities elsewhere, while others stated that they had been sent away to die. Their doubts dissipated when a young pharmacist named Bachner, who had been transferred to the Belzec death camp, escaped and returned to Krakow. His tales about Jews being stripped, shaven, and then taken to gas chambers brought the Holocaust's reality to their midst.

The Holocaust Becomes Personal to Schindler

Schindler could not ignore the horrors that surrounded his world forever. He had already begun supplementing his workers' daily food supply, but that was more out of business practicality than humane considerations. Little by little, the man who preferred happy times and long nights began to notice what he had been trying so hard to avoid— that Nazi rule subjected human beings to atrocious conditions.

The deluge of *Aktionen* by Nazi soldiers, particularly those carried out by Hitler's elite forces, the *Schützstaffel* (SS), took more Jews away from Krakow every week. Schindler initially objected to these raids because they hampered his efforts to produce mess kits, but as more individuals disappeared, he began to see the human toll. These were men and women he knew by name.

Schindler did everything in his power to protect his workers from *Aktionen*—the organized removal of Jews from the ghettos to the death camps.

The SS also angered Schindler by continually stopping groups of his workers as they marched to Emalia and forcing them to shovel snow or carry out some other minor task. Schindler complained to a Nazi official that as many as sixty workers sometimes failed to appear for work, but the official replied that there was nothing he could do because the SS had Hitler's personal approval to do almost anything they desired. When Schindler angrily mentioned that they harmed the German war effort and should be removed, the official laughed. "Get rid of them?

They're the bastards who're on top."[9] A frustrated Schindler realized that, to operate Emalia profitably, he needed to have easy access to his workers.

Since at any moment SS guards could enter Emalia to inspect the factory or bother his Jews, Schindler employed his vast powers of persuasion or resorted to bribery to shield his workers from harm. One time, three SS arrived without warning. While they walked about the factory amid hushed Jewish workers, the men debated whether a Jew was lower than an animal. One of the SS removed his pistol, stopped at a machine, and ordered a worker to eat the wood and metal sweepings that had collected on the floor nearby. The frightened worker did as ordered—for not to meant instant death—and swallowed a handful of material. "You see what I mean," said the SS. "They eat anything at all. Even an animal would never do that."[10]

Another incident that personalized the Holocaust for Schindler happened when an SS officer spotted a Jewish worker who appeared depressed. When the German asked why, Schindler explained that the man's wife and child had been taken from the ghetto in an *Aktion* and that he missed them. The officer said he would be happy to reunite the Jew with his family, and as he walked away he ordered his adjutant (assistant) to shoot the worker. As a stunned Schindler watched, the adjutant shouted for the Jew to lower his pants to his ankles and begin walking away through the factory. Schindler hurriedly attempted to talk the man out of shooting his worker, at first claiming that such an act would demoralize the other laborers and cause a decline in productivity. When that argument failed to convince the man, Schindler offered the adjutant a bottle of expensive liquor if he would not shoot his worker. The ploy worked, and the adjutant walked away while the Jewish worker nervously, but with relief, returned to his station. Schindler may have saved the man's life for the good of his business, but he could not help but be moved by the sight of an individual he knew being subjected to such terror.

In direct contrast to the SS, Schindler always treated his workers with decency. He forged an unspoken agreement with the Jews: If they kept

The Star of David

In Nazi-controlled Europe, Jews were forced to wear the Star of David on their clothing to signify that they were Jewish. Although the Nazis intended it to be a mark of shame, the Star of David carried deep significance for Jewish men and women. The symbol supposedly replicated the shape of the shield of King David, one of Israel's most revered leaders from ancient times. Made of two intertwining triangles, the Star of David came into widespread use in the seventeenth century, when Jews placed the star on buildings used as synagogues. In 1987, people who strove to establish a Jewish homeland in Israel adopted the symbol for their cause.

money pouring in to Emalia, he would protect them from the Nazis. Jews in other factories faced beatings, and his men and women feared for their lives every moment they lived in the ghetto, but they knew that once they entered Schindler's Emalia, they were safe. Somehow, Schindler kept the Nazis away from them and gave them a sense of hope that they would one day emerge from the war alive and well.

Edith Liebgold and a few other Jewish women stood inside the ghetto one day when Abraham Bankier asked if they would like to work for Oskar Schindler, whom he described as a good man. Liebgold and the others agreed, and when they arrived at Emalia, Schindler greeted them. "I

wanted to welcome you. You'll be safe working here. If you work here, then you'll live through the war."[11]

Trouble with Authorities

To acquire food for his workers and items with which to bribe Nazi guards and officials, Schindler increased his dealings on the black market. He exchanged excess pots and pans produced at Emalia for fine wines, alcohol, tobacco, and other items. He then used those commodities to gain more military contracts or to keep the SS off his back. This made good business sense to him—if he wanted to make money, he had to spend some.

Schindler flirted with danger with his actions on the black market and his

Schindler (center) was adept at schmoozing and bribing Nazi officials to get what he wanted. Here he entertains SS officials in 1942.

friendliness toward the Jews. Even though he was well acquainted with a number of high-placed German officials in both the Abwehr and the German Armaments Inspectorate, he could be apprehended for either offense. All it took was for one envious or angry individual to be upset with something he did and Schindler could disappear into the Nazi prison system.

Schindler's luck soon ran out. He was arrested near the end of 1941 and charged with dealing on the black market, an offense that could result in death. Two members of Hitler's secret police, the Gestapo, walked into Emalia and asked Schindler to accompany them to headquarters. Before he left, Schindler handed his secretary a list of officials to contact.

The influence of Schindler's Nazi friends guaranteed him better treatment. Instead of placing him in a dreary cell, the Gestapo took Schindler to the SS building and detained him in a small bedroom. His secretary appeared later in the day with toiletries, books, and a pair of pajamas, and Schindler sat down and waited while the officials arranged his release. The following morning, after Schindler ate a decent breakfast, an SS auditor entered his room to inform him that he had examined his books and found no irregularities. He added that the SS had decided to drop any further inquiries because of Schindler's connections and that he was free to go.

However, a second arrest came on April 28, 1942. During a party for Schindler's thirty-fourth birthday, Schindler absent-mindedly kissed a Jewish girl on the cheek, a criminal act in those days. The Gestapo arrived the next morning and again drove him to jail. This time, Schindler spent five days under arrest before influential associates arranged his release.

In many ways, Schindler saw little difference between his current situation and that of his motorcycle-racing period. He loved danger, but he had confidence that he would always avoid harm. Keeping his Jewish workforce safe and healthy made money for Schindler, but it also made him a potential target for any official he irritated. This became even more evident in mid-1942, when Schindler intensified his actions to protect Emalia's Jews.

Chapter Three

"Everything in My Power"

Oskar Schindler continued to make money as the Holocaust spread throughout Europe. He had been able to overlook the realities of the day—that Jews were murdered—because he buried himself in his work and because he chose not to notice. He may have been forever content to ignore the events that swirled around him had life gone on in Krakow as it had from 1939 to early 1942, but that was not to be the case. Schindler could no longer turn away from evil.

Bankier's Arrest

The first event that significantly changed Schindler's perspective of the Holocaust involved the man who helped arrange financing for Schindler's factory, Abraham Bankier. On June 3, 1942, Bankier, who had been working as a manager in Schindler's office, left the Krakow ghetto but forgot to carry with him the blue card that identified him as an essential worker in Schindler's factory. Before he arrived at Emalia, the Gestapo stopped Bankier and arrested him when he could not produce the card. They took Bankier to the train station and shoved him into a boxcar packed with other Jews to be shipped to the Auschwitz death camp. One of Schindler's secretaries saw this and telephoned her boss.

Schindler sped to the station to save his friend before the train left. He approached the young officer in charge and asked that Bankier be released because of his occupation. When the officer refused, Schindler warned that he had influential friends who could, upon contact, not only arrange Bankier's freedom but also issue orders for the SS officer to be transferred to the bitter fighting along the Russian front. "I believe I can guarantee you, that you'll be in southern Russia within the week,"[12] threatened Schindler.

As he spoke, Schindler caught a glimpse of Bankier in one of the box-cars, elbowing for space and staring out with a look of terror. The image of his friend struggling inside the confines of the crowded boxcar haunted Schindler. No longer was the Holocaust a distant event that involved faceless individuals; he had now witnessed it in a very real, personal manner.

Fortunately, Schindler's persuasive skills, combined with the possibility of being sent into combat, convinced the young officer to release Bankier. Before he opened the boxcar door, however, the officer turned to Schindler and muttered that the temporary freedom of one Jew meant little to him; it was only a matter of time before the system would capture and destroy Bankier.

Schindler used his gift for persuasion to save his factory manager from being deported to the Auschwitz death camp, where he would surely have met the same tragic fate as these Jews being boarded onto boxcars.

The Key Event: The June 4, 1942, Liquidation

Only one day later, June 4, another action so graphically portrayed the horrors of the Holocaust that Schindler knew he must take an active role in opposing it. He and his mistress, Ingrid, were taking a leisurely morning ride in the hills overlooking Krakow's ghetto. As the couple rode above the city, laughing and enjoying the fresh air, large numbers of soldiers marched into a portion of the ghetto below and began forcing Jews into the streets. Schindler watched as entire families trudged outside each apartment building and silently formed into long lines. As his eyes widened in amazement, he saw Nazi soldiers dump the contents of luggage onto the sidewalks, club Jews to death, and shoot them from close range. Vicious Doberman Pinschers growled at the Jews, and suitcases filled with valuables burst out of apartment windows to crash on the streets below.

A group of soldiers ran into one apartment building looking for Jews who had remained in what they hoped were secure hiding locations behind dresser drawers, in attics, or under beds. The Nazis, though, had more experience in this matter and knew where to look, and soon other lines of people filtered onto the streets, prodded along by the bloodthirsty Dobermans and armed soldiers. Once outside, the Nazis shot every Jew they pried out of a hiding spot. One mother huddled in fear with her young son, who appeared to Schindler to be no more than eight

Krakow

Krakow, a thriving center of Polish culture that housed a quarter-million people in 1939, was one of the nation's oldest cities. A crucial segment of its society were the sixty thousand Jews that resided in the town when World War II began. However, as Hitler rose to power in the 1930s, they became the subjects of vandalism and insults. The city served as the capital of German-controlled Poland in October 1939, when the organized persecution of the Jews began in earnest.

After herding most of the town's Jews into the ghetto, the Nazis systematically started to deport Jews to death camps at Belzec and Auschwitz-Birkenau. Jews inside the ghetto did not quietly acquiesce. They staged a December 1943 uprising that killed eleven Germans and wounded thirteen. However, fewer than one thousand of the sixty thousand Jewish residents in Krakow would survive the various deportations.

years old, while soldiers stepped toward them. In an instant, almost before Schindler grasped what was happening, a Nazi shot the mother in the neck; a second soldier pinned the boy's head to the pavement with his boot, placed the barrel of his gun against the back of his neck, and shot him.

Schindler spotted amid this carnage a little girl dressed in a red coat and cap. She slowly moved through the throngs, almost as if the guards failed to notice her existence, observing the deaths and beatings that surrounded her. However, when the boy and his mother were executed, she froze. The image unnerved Schindler to such an extent that he slipped off his horse, fell to his knees, leaned against a tree, and barely avoided vomiting.

The grotesque sequence of events that unfolded convinced Schindler that Hitler intended to eradicate every Jew from Europe. He could no longer remain an uninvolved spectator. "Beyond this day," Schindler later said, "no thinking person could fail to see what would happen. I was now resolved to do everything in my power to defeat the system."[13]

Schindler Against the Nazis

In little ways, Schindler immediately started to do what he could. To keep the elderly and the young children—the least physically strong individuals and thus prime candidates for liquidation—from being shipped to death camps, he falsified his factory records so that his older Jews were younger than they actually were and children were three or four years older. He asked Bankier and Itzhak Stern to make sure that the Emalia rosters listed a special skill for each man and woman that made them essential to the factory's productivity, and therefore less likely to be taken away.

He also warned families about impending *Aktionen*. One day, Schindler walked up to two factory workers, Richard and Lola Krumholtz, and told them that he had arranged with authorities for them to remain in Emalia that night instead of returning to the ghetto. The couple later learned that, while they had stayed at Emalia, soldiers had rounded up all their neighbors in the ghetto (none of them workers in Schindler's factory) and shipped them to death camps.

Schindler soon took even greater actions to battle the Nazi regime. Shortly after helping the Krumholtz couple, Schindler actively participated with an anti-Nazi organization. In late 1942, agents for a Zionist group (people who favored the establishment of a Jewish homeland in Palestine) secretly contacted Schindler and asked if he would travel to Budapest, Hungary, to provide information about Nazi criminal actions against the Jews in Poland. Schindler agreed, sneaked out of Poland in a baggage train, told the Jewish group what had been occurring in the Krakow

SS men pile up the bloodied victims of a brutal shooting action. Schindler resolved to do more after watching in horror such a shooting in 1942.

region and in the nearby labor camp at Plaszow, and then returned with money to deliver to Jewish underground leaders in Poland. Schindler agreed to the risky operation partly because he had always loved flirting with danger and partly because he felt he had to do something to help his workers.

Amon Goeth Arrives

Schindler's decision to take an active role was followed by the February 13,

1943, arrival in Krakow of SS captain Amon Leopold Goeth, the new commandant of the Plaszow labor camp. A sadistic individual given orders to complete the removal of all Jews from Krakow, Goeth entered Plaszow with his two killer dogs, Rolf and Ralf, who lunged at Jews on command. Goeth had joined the Nazi Party in 1930, and gradually rose through the chain of command. He had gained the attention of his superiors because of the efficient and ruthless manner with which he supervised the liquidation of the Jews living near Lublin, so they now placed him in charge of carrying out a similar program in Krakow.

Schindler and Goeth shared much in common. Though both were raised Catholic, they rarely practiced their religion. Both had concentrated on engineering, physics, and mathematics in high school, both joined the Nazi Party, both loved women and alcohol, and both had traveled to Krakow to make money—Schindler with his factory and Goeth in the black market. Goeth differed in his love of brutality—without remorse he could shoot a Jewish inmate as readily as he squashed a bug. Schindler could never harm an individual, but an odd bond formed between the two, who frequently sang, drank, and partied the nights away. Thomas Keneally, author of the book

Inmate slave laborers in the quarry at Plaszow forced-labor camp in Poland.

Goeth

Amon Leopold Goeth was born in 1908 in Vienna, Austria. He was attracted to Hitler's doctrine at an early age, joining a Nazi youth group in 1925 and the Nazi Party five years later. In February 1943, he arrived at Plaszow, where he quickly instituted his brutal reign of terror. Camp inmates learned to be alert at all times, for they never knew when Goeth and his rifle might suddenly appear.

Near the end of the war, Goeth was captured by soldiers of U.S. general George Patton's Third Army and imprisoned at Dachau. The Polish government placed him on trial for his actions, found him guilty for the deaths of more than twenty thousand people, and hanged him in Krakow on September 13, 1946. An ardent Nazi to the end, Goeth went to his death with a Nazi salute.

Schindler's List, wrote that "Amon was Oskar's dark brother, was the berserk and fanatic executioner Oskar might, by some unhappy reversal of appetites, have become."[14]

The two saw each other as a means of furthering their respective interests. Goeth wanted money; Schindler, on the other hand, hoped to keep his factory profitable while also shielding his Jews from harm. Goeth knew that Schindler, who had already bribed other Nazi officials to obtain military contracts, would freely part with some of his immense fortune to ensure that business went on as usual.

Though Schindler treated Goeth as a friend, in reality it was only a superb acting performance by an outstanding salesman. According to Itzhak Stern and other Jews, Schindler despised the brutal Goeth. Schindler's wife, Emilie, who attended a few functions at which Goeth was present, wrote, "Goeth was the most despicable man I have ever met in my whole life."[15]

Goeth wasted no time in enacting his horrid plans for Krakow, and set March 13 as the date for the final removal of all Jews from the ghetto. Schindler learned of his plans when Goeth boasted of them at one of their numerous parties. Schindler said nothing until March 12, then surprisingly ordered his Jewish workers to remain at the factory that night rather than return to the ghetto and face potential death. While his Jews huddled safe in the confines of Emalia, the SS stormed into the ghetto, collected the remaining residents, executed anyone found hiding, and transported them to death camps or to the nearby labor camp at Plaszow. At least two thousand Jews died in the liquidation, while another eight thousand entered the gates of Plaszow and Goeth's iron rule, including Schindler's Jewish workers.

Life at Plaszow

Krakow's ghetto had never given the Jews a feeling of security, but compared to Plaszow and Amon Goeth it was a paradise. At its height, Plaszow housed twenty-five thousand Jews, who every day lived in fear for their lives. One of Goeth's favorite pastimes was to wake up each morning, step out with a rifle to the porch that looked out over the camp below, and randomly shoot Jews as they worked or walked about the camp. No one ever knew when a fatal bullet might strike them.

Helen Sternlicht, a teenage Jewish girl who was Goeth's housemaid at Plaszow, recalled the absolute fear that encompassed the camp. Goeth habitually beat her for not ironing his shirts properly or for committing other minor infractions. The image of his two attack dogs haunted her for years. "He used to call me in the yard to bring out his quilted heavy gloves," Sternlicht recalled years later. "He used to put them on and train the dogs to attack people. He would call out the name—Ralf!—and the dog would run and chase people."[16]

One day, Sternlicht watched Goeth argue with a Jew. "He didn't like something about him [the Jew]. He let his two dogs go loose, and they started to tear him apart."[17] Goeth stood by as the dogs ripped chunks of flesh from the man, then ended the torment with a bullet to the man's head. In a gruesome contrast to the violence, most nights Goeth relaxed from the day's killings by listening to lullabies performed by two Plaszow inmates, brothers Henry and Leopold Rosner.

Goeth also hosted elaborate dinners at his huge Plaszow villa. Goeth and his guests, which usually included Schindler, enjoyed sumptuous feasts before sitting down to after-dinner drinks and lively debate. As usual, Schindler frequently dominated the conversation and enjoyed being the center of attention. The other guests looked forward to Schindler's attendance, for a group of beautiful women often accompanied the fun-loving businessman.

Helen Sternlicht, who had to clean up after the affairs, recalled that Schindler appeared at numerous parties, often with different women. Schindler would often chat with Sternlicht. If Goeth had humiliated Sternlicht in front of the crowd, Schindler would step into the kitchen to comfort her. "He patted my hair. He called me 'young child.'"[18]

Schindler attended these functions despite his distaste for Amon Goeth. He acted friendly toward the brutal commandant because the Nazi, upon whom Schindler bestowed numerous bribes of jewelry, expensive coats, and

Amon Goeth surveys prisoners from his porch overlooking the camp. A sadistic killer, Goeth was known to shoot prisoners at random from this vantage point.

liquor, could make life more comfortable and profitable for him. He also knew that, to help his workers, he had to develop close bonds with Goeth.

For instance, one day Goeth announced that he intended to move Emalia inside the confines of the Plaszow concentration camp. Schindler embarked on an impassioned argument to persuade Goeth not to take such an action. He claimed that a move would so disrupt his operations that produc-tivity would suffer, and German soldiers fighting on the front lines would fail to receive the materials they required. He also added that his heavy machinery would prove so difficult to move and, once in Plaszow, would require such arduous balancing adjustments that he would have to shut down factory output for too long. Then, as Goeth knew would happen, Schindler backed up his persuasiveness with more bribes. Goeth accepted Schindler's

Plaszow

The Nazis constructed Plaszow from the destroyed remains of two Jewish cemeteries on Krakow's outskirts. They cleared the Krakowski and Podgorski cemeteries and then fashioned the camp's concrete roads from crushed gravestones.

Besides Plaszow's Jews, the concentration camp housed Polish dissidents, Gypsies, and German criminals. The inmates produced uniforms and other items needed by the German military, and worked in a nearby stone quarry. Conditions worsened in 1944 when the camp commander received orders to concentrate on liquidating the inmates, but he was stopped from completing his task by the approaching Soviet army. The Nazis attempted to hide traces of their atrocities by digging up and burning the buried remains of the inmates who had been killed and by relocating the surviving Jews to other camps. In September 1944, the Plaszow camp closed after its final inmates were sent to Auschwitz-Birkenau.

Plaszow inmates toil under the watchful eye of camp guards.

Schindler (left, at a party with SS officers) used his charm and charisma to fool officials into believing that he was in full support of the Nazi cause.

bribes, and Emalia remained outside Plaszow.

Schindler's most important work on behalf of his Jewish workers had barely begun, however. His greatest challenges lay in the last year of the war, when he put to use his gift for talking and for delivering desirable items. As a result, eleven hundred men and women survived who might have died in Plaszow, Auschwitz, or any of the other death camps.

Chapter Four

"Who Works for Me, Lives"

By the end of 1942, Oskar Schindler preferred business and pleasure above everything else. He loved making money, and he enjoyed spending it even more. That changed as Nazi oppression placed increasingly heavy burdens on the Jewish workers in his factory and as fear and terror widened. Seeing this, Schindler took bolder action to improve the lives of his laborers. No longer content to help with consoling words, Schindler created a safe haven for his people behind the walls of his factory.

"His Brilliant Eloquence"

A mixture of business concerns and humanitarianism prodded Schindler into taking more active steps to ensure the safety of his laborers. He and other Krakow businessmen who depended on Jewish workers complained to Amon Goeth that their people so often arrived late from Plaszow camp that output had suffered. On some days, Schindler waited hours for his workforce, which had usually been detained somewhere along the route from Plaszow to Emalia by a Nazi officer who forced them to remove trash or snow; many were also ordered to remain in Plaszow to witness one of the numerous hangings or beatings. When they finally walked through the doors of Emalia, the Jews could not work as efficiently because of the state of shock they were in over what they had experienced.

Schindler also worried that in Plaszow, fear and danger constantly surrounded his Jews. He controlled the situation while they worked at Emalia, but once the workday ended, the men and women returned to Goeth's iron grip. At any moment, Goeth or a camp guard could end one of his laborer's lives. Schindler despised the lack of control he had over his Jews, both on account of their safety and because of how it affected Emalia's profits.

Schindler spoke to influential officials in and outside of the German military in hopes of alleviating the situation. He made Emalia more important for the Nazis by convincing an influential general that he could cheaply produce ammunition as well as mess kits. Since Emalia would therefore be manufacturing items considered more essential to the German war effort, and since Schindler required the continuous use of Jews from Plaszow camp, Nazi officials declared Plaszow a war-essential concentration camp rather than a labor camp. This change in designation did not alleviate harsh conditions inside Plaszow, but it at least guaranteed that Goeth's camp would not be readily dismantled and its occupants shipped to nearby Auschwitz, as was steadily occurring in other labor camps.

As usual, Schindler's combination of persuasion and bribery helped Nazi officials to make the changes. Whenever he wanted something, Schindler traveled to Nazi headquarters in Krakow, or even the German capital in Berlin, armed with flowery words, compliments, money, and alcohol. More often than not, he departed with papers ordering his requests.

As Schindler's demands increased, the cost of working with the Nazis skyrocketed as well. Schindler realized

Jewish Resistance

Jewish residents of the Krakow ghetto may have been in a near-hopeless situation, but it did not prevent many from mounting heroic resistance to their Nazi tormentors. Underground organizations flourished. Some focused on organizing assistance for residents, and one published a newspaper called the *Fighting Pioneer*.

In October 1942 a group of young Jewish prisoners established the Jewish Fighting Organization. The men conducted armed resistance outside the ghetto. They quickly struck local targets such as supplies of weapons or electrical lines and then disappeared back into the ghetto. The most renowned operation targeted a Krakow café that catered to German officers. The Jewish fighters killed eleven Nazis and wounded thirteen.

Female office workers pose outside Emalia. Schindler increasingly risked his own life and livelihood to protect his workers from harm.

that he could completely protect his workers from harm only when they remained under his control at all times, so he decided to approach Goeth and other officials with an audacious request. He asked that he be allowed to construct his own camp attached to Emalia, one strictly for his Jewish workers. Such a move guaranteed the presence of his workforce, which was good for business, and it removed the people from Goeth's clutches at Plaszow. However, it would be costly, both in bribery and in purchasing the needed construction materials.

Again relying on compelling words and gifts, Schindler persuaded an engineering officer in the German Armaments Inspectorate to write a letter to Berlin supporting the idea. Bearing money, jewelry, and alcohol, he also gained the support of officials of the Nazi government in Poland. Schindler was at his best in arranging the full-time shift of his workers to Emalia; he hosted an array of parties during which he befriended influential individuals and established important contacts. His wife, Emilie, recalled of her husband, "As soon as he began

Schindler (second from left) hosted parties for Nazi officials to establish contacts, gain their confidence, and bribe them for information.

talking, everybody would listen, and he was able to convince everyone with his brilliant eloquence. He made himself look important in other people's eyes just through his conviction of his own importance."[19]

Schindler next approached Goeth, whose willingness to go along with the construction of Schindler's subcamp had been eased by Plaszow's earlier designation as a war-essential camp. Since Berlin deemed Plaszow more important to the war effort, the camp commander's status increased in similar proportion. Schindler found little opposition to the move when he first mentioned it to Goeth; however, the camp commander let Schindler know that he expected bribes to rise in accordance with his newfound status.

The Emalia Subcamp

To begin construction on the subcamp, Schindler first had to purchase the adjoining land, which was owned by an elderly couple named Bielski. Rather than waste time haggling over the price, Schindler offered the Bielskis a price they would normally have seen only in the brisk economic days before the war. When the couple agreed to sell the land, Schindler immediately called his lawyers to draw up the legal papers. He then used a huge portion of

Emalia's profits to finance the costly move. Schindler made almost $5 million in 1943, but much of his fortune now went to bribery, daily expenses, and the new camp.

The Emalia subcamp drained Schindler's monetary supply. Though Goeth agreed to let Schindler construct what amounted to his own concentration camp, the Nazi commandant demanded that Emalia be built according to SS guidelines. Nine-foot fences, liberally sprinkled with watchtowers containing armed guards, surrounded Emalia. Six new barracks, designed to house twelve hundred workers, anchored the complex, which also included a

medical and dental clinic, a bathhouse to ensure cleanliness and protect against disease, a delousing complex, a barbershop, one store, a laundry, and latrines. The enormous cost for this project came from Schindler's own pocket, but he took comfort in knowing that at least his workers would be safer than they would if they remained in Plaszow.

The Jews immediately recognized the difference between Emalia and Plaszow, even though they still lived behind barbed-wire fences and stared at armed Nazi guards. Emalia had no permanent commandant comparable to Plaszow's Goeth—Schindler bore the responsibility

Unlike at Plaszow (pictured), where inmates lived in constant fear for their lives, prisoners at Schindler's Emalia subcamp were never subjected to beatings or shootings.

for governing the complex—so daily beatings or shootings never occurred. The guards remained at their posts along the fence or inside the factory rather than wandering at will throughout the camp. Schindler also arranged for the guards to be switched every two days so that they would not develop personal bitterness toward any Jews and thus seek to harm them. If a guard tried to mistreat the inmates or wanted to inspect the camp, a speedy telephone call from Schindler to his superior resulted in the offending individual being replaced. Schindler rarely had to worry about this, though, because the Nazi guards considered working at Emalia, with its better food and easy duty, a soft assignment.

The camp contained two barbed-wire passageways: one that led from the workers' barracks to the enamelware section of the factory and a second that took workers to the munitions portion. The Jews continued to work twelve hours a day, for Schindler still intended to turn a profit, but no one collapsed from overwork or from beatings. Thomas Keneally, the author of *Schindler's List*, wrote, "Though the SS may have set the limits to the life people led in Emalia, Oskar set its tone. There were no dogs. There were no beatings."[20]

A Nazi Without a Gun

Schindler took extra steps to make life at Emalia as pleasant as possible. Although he could not free the workers from Nazi rule, he could at least soften the impact and reduce the misery. Schindler purchased large supplies of food and medicine from the black market to supplement the few hundred loaves of bread and watery soup shipped over each week by the Plaszow bakery.

Despite a Nazi rule forbidding Jews from smoking, Schindler loved to walk through his factory, light a cigarette, and then toss it to the ground and walk away so a nearby worker could enjoy a smoke. He often opened a new pack of cigarettes, lit one, placed the pack on a machine or workbench while he supposedly inspected the work area, and then walked away without taking the pack. He repeated this as he strolled among the machines, making sure to leave plenty of cigarettes for his workers. Sometimes, Schindler left more than cigarettes. He frequently offered encouraging words to boost morale, and occasionally managed to leave sandwiches lying about.

Schindler did not have to worry about guards making unannounced inspections, but other SS officials from Krakow or Berlin could barge in unexpectedly to check on the quality of work or to search for illegal items in the workers' barracks. To prevent these surprise inspections, Schindler installed wiring that led from his office to a bell in the barracks. If a high-level bureaucrat from the Armaments Inspectorate or an SS officer arrived to examine the

SS officers led by Heinrich Himmler inspect inmates at Dachau concentration camp. Schindler used gifts and bribes to deflect officials who dropped in at Emalia for unannounced inspections.

barracks, Schindler pushed a button to warn his workers to extinguish any cigarettes and to return to their own bunks.

Schindler also used his charm to deflect sudden inspections or demands that his Jewish workers be deported to a death camp. Itzhak Stern, who worked in the office with Schindler, remembered their routine being continually interrupted by inspectors:

Almost every day, from morning until evening, "controls" visitors and commissions came to the factory and made me nervous. Schindler used to keep pouring them vodka and joking with them. When they left he would ask me in, close the door and then quietly tell me whatever they had come for. He used to tell them that he knew how to get work out of these Jews and that he wanted more brought in. That was how we managed to get in the families and relatives all the time and save them from deportation.[21]

Schindler saved many Jews accused of crimes by arguing that their death would hamper his efforts to produce essential war products. Taking out a fresh bottle of cognac or gently nudging a piece of jewelry into their pockets, Schindler mentioned that they could always deal with the Jew later, but right now the war effort needed his or her labor. The Nazi in question usually departed without further argument.

One time, two Gestapo agents arrived and demanded that Schindler hand over five workers who had forged travel papers. Schindler took the men into his office, started telling stories as he poured vodka, and sent the men on their way without the Jews they had come for. As he explained after the war, "Three hours after they walked in, two drunken Gestapo men reeled out of my office without their prisoners and without the incriminating documents they had demanded."[22]

During another inspection, Rena Ferber was laboring over a large press when the machine broke down. The Nazi guard accused her of purposely sabotaging the item and threatened to take her away. "I became the center of attention," explained Ferber, "and the thing to be in camp was *not* to be, and just to blend in. I was terrified." Before the guard could remove her, Schindler walked up, looked at the machine, and convinced the guard that Ferber could not possibly have enough knowledge or strength to have damaged the machine. The guard departed. "He [Schindler] was very dashing. He made

me think of Clark Gable. He winked at me."[23]

On another occasion, Schindler and Goeth drove alongside a group of cattle cars packed with Jews waiting to be shipped to the Mauthausen death camp. The plaintive cries for water that emitted from the stifling cars moved Schindler to ask Goeth if he could have the cars hosed down with water. Goeth assented, so Schindler gathered a group of Jewish workers nearby, located a hose, and doused the cars so thoroughly that enough water leaked inside for the occupants to quench their thirst.

One of the Jews asked to water down the cars, Murray Pantirer, recalled that Schindler "got permission from Goeth, and he ordered some of us boys to stretch a hose to the cars and soak them with water. You see it in the movie [Steven Spielberg's *Schindler's List*], with the hoses, except we had garden hoses. To me it was unbelievable, a Nazi with the [party lapel] pin, but no gun or uniform. And I saw his convertible full of cigarettes and whiskey and chocolate. He was dressed so elegantly, in a white suit."[24]

Schindler also bribed an officer so that each time the train halted on its journey, guards would open the doors to allow air inside and place cans of water in each car. Survivors from this train later claimed that Schindler's kindness gave them enough strength to endure the horrendous trip and subsequent incarceration in Mauthausen.

"You're Going to Be Free from That Hell"

The events of the Holocaust robbed people of their everyday security. Victims no longer felt safe and sheltered, for any moment could be their last. With Schindler, however, that sense of security returned. In Emalia, although they might have worked long hours and seen barbed-wire fences, they did not suddenly disappear or collapse under a guard's truncheon. Jews in

Plaszow knew that if they could somehow join Schindler's oasis at Emalia, they stood a fair chance of surviving the war. As one mentioned, "By Schindler, we were hungry, but not starving. We were cold, but not freezing. We had fear, but we were not beaten."[25]

Moshe Bejski was one of the fortunate Jews to leave the squalor of Plaszow for Emalia. "There was no killing whatsoever in the Schindler camp," he said.

In Plaszow hardly a day passed when there were no killings. Every

The workers Schindler saved later called themselves *Schindlerjuden*—"Schindler's Jews." At center, he poses with some of his grateful employees at a reunion in 1946.

German could kill at will. Schindler's people didn't work as hard as we worked in Plaszow. We worked fourteen to eighteen hours a day. Schindler provided supplementary food for his workers. An extra half loaf of bread was very important in those times. Schindler was supposed to be making kitchenware for the army, but he sold part of it on the black market [for food and medical supplies].[26]

Most of the Jews who worked for Schindler, who later called themselves *Schindlerjuden*—"Schindler's Jews"— speak of their benefactor in revered, almost biblical tones. They compare Emalia to heaven and depict Schindler as a modern-day Moses leading his people to safety, a notion Schindler reinforced with his comments.

Helen Sternlicht, a young Jewish girl who worked as Goeth's maid, frequently saw Schindler at Goeth's numerous dinners and parties. One day, Schindler walked into the room where she worked, asked her to look out the window at the Jews below who were lifting heavy boulders under the watchful eye of Nazi guards, and promised he would save her. "You see people in Egypt, the Jewish people when they were slaves," he mentioned to Sternlicht, "and then they were freed from Egypt. That's what's going to happen to you, you will see. You're going to be free from that hell."[27]

Schindler lifted the Jews from despair and gave his people hope. The *Schindlerjuden*, aware of Schindler's many relationships with beautiful women, said they were thankful he was more faithful about his promises to them than he was to Emilie. Edith Wertheim's first sight of Emalia's owner restored her belief in goodness. When she arrived at Emalia, "I saw a handsome, *gorgeous* man—I really was struck by how beautiful he was. I saw a good face, smiling at us. I was not scared. He said, 'Children, don't worry. Who works for me, lives through the war.'"[28]

When the movie *Schindler's List* premiered years later, Steven Spielberg invited Wertheim and other *Schindlerjuden* to a party after a special screening of the film. Wertheim met the actor who portrayed Schindler, the handsome Liam Neeson, who gave Wertheim a big hug and kiss. Wertheim responded, "You know what? You are gorgeous, but you're still not Oskar Schindler!"[29]

"I Did What . . . My Conscience Told Me"

To this day, people, including the *Schindlerjuden*, have no definitive answer to why Schindler, who so loved luxury, placed himself in such danger and went to such great expense to help people. A handful of critics claim that he kept his Jews alive so he could profit from their labor. If that is the case, then why did he so freely expend his fortune, and why did he add to his fac-

Actor Liam Neeson portrayed the handsome, charming Schindler in the 1993 Steven Spielberg film *Schindler's List*.

tory roster many young and elderly individuals who could not possibly have put in a full day's work?

Some people believe that Schindler experienced a gradual evolution in attitude, that he started out with nothing but profit in mind but wound up concerned for the safety of his people. Bronia Gunz, a *Schindlerjude*, said, "My opinion is that in the beginning, he didn't know the Jews existed. He was a Nazi. But when he took us to Emalia, he started to speak to us and started to see some intelligence in us. He started to feel sorry for us when he saw Goeth shooting us. He saw we were nice, hard-working people, and they were killing us only because we were born Jewish. He had a change of heart."[30]

Others point out that Schindler, the former motorcycle racer, loved the thrill of the hunt and helped his Jews simply to see if he could get away with it, to see if he could save people right under the noses of the Nazi tormentors. Some argue that Schindler did not know why, but simply reacted to a terrible situation.

When asked after the war by some *Schindlerjuden* why he acted the way he did, Schindler usually had no answer or quickly changed the topic. To one query, though, he remarked that he had acted as if he had seen a dog about to be run over by a car—that he would stop to save the creature from harm. "I hated the brutality, the sadism, and the insanity of Nazism," said Schindler. "I just couldn't stand by and see people destroyed. I did what I could, what I had to do, what my conscience told me I must do. That's all there is to it. Really, nothing more."[31]

Moshe Bejski concluded that one had to accept that Schindler had a con-

Despite his flaws, Schindler was foremost a hero to the many Jews he saved during the war.

fusing array of attitudes and motives but that in the end all that mattered was that he saved people:

Schindler was a drunkard, Schindler was a womanizer. His relations with his wife were rather bad. Each time he had not one but several girlfriends. So, I am aware of who Schindler was, but without Schindler most of those 1,200 Jews would not have remained alive, certainly not as a group. You had to take him as he was. Schindler was a very complex person. Schindler was a good human being. He was against evil. He acted spontaneously.[32]

Poldek Pfefferberg, who later played a crucial role in bringing Schindler's story to book and film, summarized the attitude of most *Schindlerjuden*. When a reporter asked him in 1993 why Schindler helped, Pfefferberg abruptly stated that he did not care what his motivations were. "Who cares! I don't give a hoot for the reasons he did it. He saved eleven hundred people."[33]

As the war moved through 1944, conditions soured around Emalia. To the east, the Soviet army gradually moved closer as it pushed the German military out of Russia and back toward Germany. Realizing that the Russian army would soon uncover evidence of the concentration camp system, Nazi authorities ordered some camps closed and declared that the bodies of dead Jews, which had been buried, must be unearthed and burned to eliminate any signs of their actions in the death camps.

Schindler spoke of the events to Henry Rosner. As he talked, Schindler suddenly picked up his office chair, walked to the mandatory picture of Hitler that adorned his wall, and thought of smashing the chair into it before regaining his composure. "They're burning bodies out there, aren't they?"[34] he asked Rosner.

He needed no answer, for Schindler already knew what his Nazi associates were doing. The information spurred Schindler to his greatest feat.

Chapter Five

"You're with Me Now"

As the horrors of the Nazi plan to eradicate European Jews became evident, Schindler shifted his focus. His concern for profits vanished. In its place rose a deep longing to save his workers from the fate that awaited so many Jews in Poland, Czechoslovakia, and other portions of Europe controlled by Hitler and his Nazis. Along the way, Schindler watched the immense fortune he had so carefully accumulated disappear.

Move to Czechoslovakia

By mid-1944, Germany found itself in a precarious military situation. Not only was the Soviet army encroaching from the east, but in the west, British and American forces steadily advanced from the beaches of France toward the German borders. As German units

yielded ground, Hitler and his top advisers scurried to remove traces of what had been taking place in their death camps. They started with locations in Poland, such as Plaszow, because the Soviet army threatened to smash through German lines in that region before Britain and the United States arrived near camps to the west.

Schindler learned from Goeth that he would soon have to close Emalia and transfer his Jews to Plaszow so they could be sent to other camps. By late September 1944, other Jews had already been shipped out, while the bodies of the thousands slain under Goeth had been dug out of their shallow graves and cremated. Goeth told Schindler that his male workers would be sent to Gross Rosen, a rock quarry along the Polish-Czechoslovakian border notorious for its harsh treatment and arduous work. His female workers would be shipped to Auschwitz for a speedy death in its gas chambers.

News of the impending action moved quickly through the factory. Men and women who had labored under Schindler for more than a year and had regained hope that they might have a future after the war now faced unspeakable perils once again. Many believed that Schindler, their protector through so much, could no longer keep them from death. They had forgotten how resourceful and determined he could be.

Schindler traveled to his hometown of Zwittau, intent on locating another spot for his factory. He inspected an abandoned textile plant on the outskirts of Brinnlitz, a village near Zwittau, that offered promise. Owned by a family in Vienna, the two-story building seemed to offer exactly what he needed. Schindler could turn the first floor into his factory, and his workers could occupy the second floor as a barracks.

His next steps required careful planning and a lot of money. Schindler first had to convince Goeth that the move to Czechoslovakia, where they

The ruins of a gas chamber and crematorium at Auschwitz. Near the end of the war, the Nazis destroyed many such buildings at the death camps in an effort to conceal their crimes.

could continue to make war products and be farther from the advancing Soviet army, made more sense than simply sending his Jews to apparent death in other camps. The willing Goeth, who always spotted an opportunity to obtain gifts and money from Schindler, agreed, assuming that Schindler received permission from Goeth's superiors in Berlin.

Schindler pestered every individual he knew in Berlin—again offering expensive jewelry and money. When he experienced opposition, Emilie, his long-suffering but devoted wife back home, appealed to an important official who had once been her swimming teacher in school. Finally, after many words and even more money, Schindler walked away with official approval to move his factory from Plaszow to Brinnlitz.

But Schindler still had to overcome a final hurdle. Brinnlitz's residents actively opposed the factory's opening. Not only would a factory producing essential war materials subject the region to American and British bombing, but it would bring Jews along with it. Signs stating "KEEP THE JEWISH CRIMINALS OUT" dotted area roads, and people complained to Brinnlitz town leaders.

As always, the fast-talking Schindler was prepared with a torrent of words backed up by an abundance of cash. Thousands of dollars poured out of his wallet, and Schindler once again triumphed. When the Plaszow camp closed in late September 1944, Schindler stood ready to move his people out of Poland.

A List Is Born

In preparation for the immense move, Schindler compiled what has become known around the world as "Schindler's List," a roster of names consisting of the Jews he intended to take with him. As word spread in Emalia and at Plaszow of Schindler's intentions, every Jew tried to get his or her name added to the roster.

The names came from different sources. Schindler selected some of the people, adding a special skill after their names to ensure that German authorities would not question the choice. Other Jewish names came from another local businessman who employed Jewish workers, Julius Madritsch. Madritsch, who had earned a reputation for helping his Jews in a manner similar to Schindler's, did not have the funds or connections to continue assisting his workers, but he convinced Schindler to take about seventy of his people.

Since Schindler was so absorbed in setting up the new Brinnlitz factory, which required 250 freight cars packed with equipment, he placed one of his clerks, Marcel Goldberg, in charge of finishing the list. However, Goldberg took advantage of his responsibility by demanding money or jewelry from any Jew seeking inclusion, and as a result

Motivation for Change

Much has been written about what compelled Schindler to take the extraordinary steps to save more than one thousand people. Most likely, a combination of reasons produces an appropriate answer. In *Schindler's Legacy*, her book about the *Schindlerjuden,* author Elinor J. Brecher quotes Henry Rosner as claiming that Schindler changed because of one event: Two Jewish girls who attempted to escape from Plaszow were hanged in front of him. "Schindler came and saw Goeth shoot them two seconds before they died hanging. Schindler vomited in front of everybody. He would never be working for the Germans again, he said to me."

Author Thomas Fensch, who interviewed Schindler in depth, gives another reason. In Fensch's book, *Oskar Schindler and His List,* Schindler explains that he could no longer watch the cruelty and deaths of his people, and that he felt compelled to do something. Whatever the reason or reasons, Schindler's actions saved many lives.

Schindler shows a photograph of some of the people he saved during the Holocaust.

some of Schindler's Emalia Jews were left off the final list. This produced angry outcries, but since Schindler was often out of the area on business, Goldberg's selection remained. Some of Schindler's workers blamed him for their not being placed on the list and for the subsequent deaths of loved ones, but the businessman had to spend time dining with officials, arranging transactions, and organizing briberies, so he had to leave other details to his subordinates.

Other people had no idea how they had been chosen. Maurice Markheim was as astonished as anyone when camp officials announced his name as one of the fortunate. "How did I get there?" he wondered later. "If there is a God, only God knows who put me on the list. I had no protection anymore: no diamonds, nothing!"[35]

The final list contained the names of eight hundred men and three hundred women. The move came at the right moment, for on September 13, 1944, German authorities arrested Amon Goeth on charges of involvement in the black market and confined him to a prison in Vienna, Austria. Had the arrest occurred sooner, Schindler may not have enjoyed the same relationship with a new commander that he had developed with Goeth.

"Like a Lifetime for Us"

On October 15, 1944, the eight hundred men boarded trains for what they

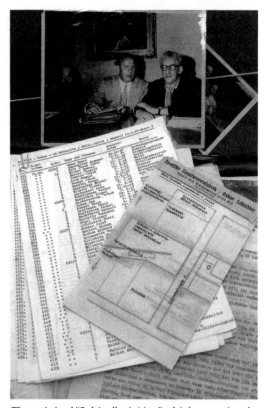

The original "Schindler's List," which contained the names of eleven hundred people Schindler intended to take with him to his new factory.

thought was a trip to Brinnlitz. To their astonishment, three days later they arrived at the Gross Rosen death camp. Brutal guards forced them off the trains to a gathering location, where the men were forced to shed their clothes. As they shivered in the cold, an overpowering stench almost sickened them. Moshe Bejski, a *Schindlerjude* who was among the group, explained, "We arrived at Gross Rosen late in the afternoon. We saw the chimneys of the crematoria burning. We weren't so sure we were going to Schindler. We were kept outside all night for a very exact body search, even internal. We were naked all night on a very cold late October night. I got my clothes at eleven o'clock the next morning."[36]

For men who only a few days before lived with the hope of being delivered from Plaszow's horrors to the safe confines of Schindler's factory in Brinnlitz, the detention at Gross Rosen served as a cruel reminder that their lives could, at any moment, be suddenly altered by the Nazis. Instead of security, they faced fear. Despair replaced hope.

"You had to open your mouth and spread the fingers and bend over and lift up your feet because you could have [something] on the bottom,"[37] said *Schindlerjude* Chaskel Schlesinger of the demeaning body searches. Guards then led the men into delousing showers to prepare them for entrance into the camp. Fortunately, a German officer who knew that these men came from Schindler spotted the eight hundred men, ordered their clothes to be returned, and had them placed in a barracks until Schindler could be notified.

The men waited three torturous weeks for rescue. Each day they watched other Jews go to their deaths and wondered whether their benefactor would come to their aid. Finally, guards marched them to the train sta-

tion, where they stepped onto trains that transported them to Brinnlitz.

The three hundred women faced an even more frightening ordeal. They left Plaszow within one week of the men, but instead of Brinnlitz or Gross Rosen, the train stopped at one of Europe's most dreaded spots—Auschwitz. Guards shoved them off the trains, stripped them of their clothes, and shaved their heads as if the women were any group of Jews being accepted for quick deaths. When the guards ordered them to step toward a building for a shower, cries emitted from some women who feared that, instead of water, deadly gas would flow down from the shower heads. The Nazi guards let them think that they were walking to their deaths, but once inside, a welcome stream of water greeted the women. Death had been postponed for the moment, but no one knew how long they could escape the dangers of Auschwitz.

Manci Rosner, one of Schindler's Jewish workers, waited in trepidation to see whether Schindler would once again save them. "That time in Auschwitz was like a lifetime for us," she said. "I am so thankful to Oskar Schindler. I never would have survived it. At least in Plaszow, no ovens, no gas. You knew when you went to the shower, you got a shower. There is no comparison [to Auschwitz]. I can only remember the smell: a terrible stench."[38]

Railroad tracks lead the way into Auschwitz-Birkenau, the largest and most infamous of the extermination camps designed to carry out the "Final Solution."

"You Have Nothing More to Worry About"

Unknown to the women, Schindler faced difficulties of his own. Shortly after the SS took Goeth away, they returned to arrest Schindler for dealing in the black market. Some suspect that Goeth, in an attempt to help his own cause, gave the SS information on Schindler's activities. Schindler lingered in jail for a week before his high-placed connections helped free him.

Back at Brinnlitz, Schindler bristled when he learned of the women's fate and instantly set about freeing them. Stories conflict as to exactly how he obtained their release, but most agree that he employed a beautiful woman to travel to Auschwitz. According to Itzhak Stern, Schindler offered the woman, whom Emilie claimed was one of Schindler's mistresses named Hilde, a large diamond if she could convince the camp commandant to release the three hundred women. "Take the list of the women," said Schindler to Hilde, "pack a suitcase with the best food and liquor you can find in my kitchen. Then go to Auschwitz. You know the Commandant has a penchant for pretty women. If you bring it off, you'll get this diamond. And more still."[39]

Apparently, the ploy failed. So Schindler headed to Auschwitz, talked to the commander, and in his usual manner arranged for his workers to be released. When trains bearing the women pulled into Brinnlitz, the relieved workers saw Schindler waiting for them. "We knew you were coming," he said to the gathering. "When you go inside the building, you'll find soup and bread waiting for you. You have nothing more to worry about. You're with me now."[40]

The women could barely contain their joy at seeing the one person who had sheltered them from the war. Within weeks they had plunged from hope to despair, only to once again face a future free from fear. "He was our father, he was our mother, he was our only faith," stated one of the women. "He never let us down."[41]

To prevent the spread of deadly typhus from the body lice that most of the women carried from Auschwitz, Schindler ordered the women deloused and had their clothes boiled. Then he placed them in barracks for a much-needed rest.

"Only the Soup of Schindler . . . Had Body"

The factory at Brinnlitz supposedly was to produce artillery shells for the German army, but Schindler had a different plan in mind. Whereas he once fretted over turning a profit, he now intended to employ his full resources in keeping his Jews alive. Brinnlitz became a haven, a refuge, rather than a valuable cog in the German military.

Won in a Card Game

The fate of Goeth's maid, Helen Hirsch, was determined in a card game. After winning a decent amount of money playing blackjack with Goeth, Schindler suggested they play one more hand. If Goeth won, Schindler would pay him double the amount he had won that night. If Schindler won, Goeth would let Schindler place Hirsch on the list of people chosen to go to Brinnlitz.

The two sat down to a final hand. According to Thomas Keneally's *Schindler's List*, when Schindler won, Goeth wrote on a piece of his official stationery, "I authorize that the name of prisoner Helen Hirsch be added to any list of skilled workers relocated with Herr Schindler's DEF Works." In return, Schindler wiped out the money owed by Goeth.

Schindler's Brinnlitz artillery factory (pictured in 2000) was built as a haven for Schindler's Jews and rarely produced usable munitions for the German army.

Rarely did Brinnlitz turn out any usable munitions for the Germans. Schindler ordered his workers to slow their pace, and whatever they completed always seemed to contain defects. Schindler earned money at Brinnlitz, but nowhere near what he had come to expect during his days at Emalia. Besides, he still had to send more than $18,000 each week to SS headquarters as payment for his workers. For the first time in his wartime career, Schindler's expenses greatly exceeded his income.

In addition to the regular payments, Schindler covered the weekly cost of purchasing extra food and medical supplies from the black market. He could not obtain choice cuts of meat or delectable fruit—few people in Europe, Jew or non-Jew, enjoyed those luxuries in wartime—but he fed his people much more than most owners of factories. As Thomas Keneally wrote in *Schindler's List*, "In all the miserable winter-bound continent, only the Jews of Brinnlitz were fed this living meal. Among the millions, only the soup of the Schindler thousand had body."[42]

Schindler never would have accomplished as much as he did at

Brinnlitz had the Nazi guards been devoted fanatics to Hitler's cause. Fortunately, the guards were older men who had been sent to relieve younger, healthier soldiers for duty on the front. Rather than rigidly enforcing the system, these men sought enough food and warm quarters, which Schindler made sure they received. He promised them easy duty, and asked in exchange only that they not interfere with his operation of Brinnlitz. Should they become too inquisitive about his operations, Schindler promised to have them on the first train headed toward the Russian front. The guards, experienced enough to know that the war was nearing an end, were more than happy to comply.

When inspectors made their periodic visits to Brinnlitz, Schindler arranged appropriate welcomes of food and alcohol. If they insisted on seeing a sample of his product, Schindler took them to a supply of workable artillery shells that he placed in his factory for just such a purpose. The Nazi inspectors checked them out, then went on their way satisfied with Brinnlitz's efficiency. To keep Berlin authorities from becoming too suspicious, Schindler interspersed small shipments of quality shells with the defective ones.

He used other tricks to fool inspectors as well. To ensure that the metal parts of products would not harden to the proper degree, the Jewish workers fixed gauges on furnaces so that they displayed higher temperatures than were actually being used. When an inspector inquired why Schindler needed a group of nine-year-old girls, Schindler quickly replied that theirs were the only hands and fingers small enough to reach into the interior of shells to clean the workings.

Emilie Arrives

For the first time in their married life, Schindler and Emilie labored together. She arrived shortly after Brinnlitz opened, and quickly became known among the workers for her compassion and kindness. She nursed people to health, comforted them in dark moments, and once traveled two hundred miles to trade two suitcases of vodka for much-needed medicines. Emilie even convinced a local wealthy German lady, Frau von Daubek, to donate grain from her grain mill.

The union reached only into their business world, however. Emilie and Oskar remained distant toward each other, mainly because Oskar continued to see other women. They owned a spectacular villa overlooking a peaceful valley near the factory, but they rarely slept in it. Schindler knew that his workers feared being taken away during the night, so he and Emilie slept on cots in his office.

The stoic wife maintained the same view she had always had—that Oskar loved her and would one day give up his other companions for her. In the meantime, she labored at the side of the man she loved on behalf of the Jews. "She [Emilie] was dominated by Oskar," explained one female worker. "As we all were. Yet she was her own woman."[43]

Similar to the situation of Schindler's mother and father, Oskar and Emilie failed to establish a familial feeling toward each other. He forged such bonds with his workers instead. The Jews viewed Schindler as a protective father, and he loved to refer to them as his "children." In effect, he created the family he never experi-

enced during his childhood and was unable or unwilling to fashion with Emilie.

"We Have Jumped into an Abyss"

Schindler's daily schedule revolved almost entirely around obtaining food and supplies to keep his people alive. As material became more scarce in the war's final months, he had to spend more time bartering on the black market. Each day he tried to purchase something to help, whether it was a supply of potatoes, some blankets, or

Schindler became a father figure to the *Schindlerjuden,* whom he sometimes referred to as his "children."

A Frozen Cattle Car

In January 1945 Schindler learned that one hundred Jews, packed into three frozen cattle cars for ten days, had arrived in Zwittau. Knowing that he had to act quickly if he hoped to save the people inside from freezing to death in the five-degree temperatures, Schindler rushed to the station and asked an official to show him the destination order for the train. As the official tended to other matters, Schindler surreptitiously altered the final destination so that it read Brinnlitz, then took charge of the frigid cargo.

With help from his Brinnlitz workers, Schindler pried open the car. So much ice had formed on the locks that the men had to use axes and then start a fire to get at the doors. Victor Lewis, a *Schindlerjude* who witnessed the event, later explained in Elinor J. Brecher's book *Schindler's Legacy:* "We took straw and burned it underneath the cars. We tried to melt the ice. Schindler said to take old mattresses—'tomorrow you get new.' When this melted and they opened the cars, people were lying on the floor, frozen."

Survivors, barely clinging to life, had stacked the bodies of four dead occupants off to one corner while they huddled against each other for warmth. Schindler and the others silently stared at the people, most of whom weighed less than a hundred pounds and had turned black from the cold. Schindler transported the survivors to Brinnlitz, emptied a room in the factory in which to place them, and gave them small amounts of warm milk and medicine. Emilie spent every waking moment caring for the group and slowly nursed them back to health. For the remainder of the war—almost six months—Schindler listed these people on his roster and paid the daily wage rate to the SS, even though they were unable to work a single day for him.

even rifles and pistols to guard against that day when the SS might try to forcibly remove the Jews.

As he catered to their physical needs, he tried to accommodate their religious ones as well. If a worker died, Schindler made sure they were buried with a religious ceremony rather than simply tossed into an unmarked grave. He also allowed the Jews to observe their special holidays, such as Hanukkah, and brought in extra food to mark the occasions.

As always, Schindler continued to help wherever he could. One time, an SS officer toured the factory and discovered that a machine would not work. He ordered the young Jew stationed at the machine to be taken away, but Schindler insisted that the man was essential to his factory. When the officer refused to listen, Schindler said he would place the young boy on trial right on the spot. He stormed out of the office, acted as if he were irate at the worker, then convicted him of breaking the machine. A screaming Schindler sentenced the youth to three weeks on the night shift as he kicked and punched at him with blows that only he and the worker knew carried half impact. Satisfied, the SS officer departed.

Schindler endangered both his life and that of his wife in taking these steps to help his workers. One day, Emilie, who was so shaken by the many close calls that she smoked up to forty cigarettes each day, wondered how much longer the difficult times would last. Her husband turned to her and replied, "My dear Emilie, we have jumped into an abyss. There is no turning back."[44]

To the everlasting gratefulness of his Jews, Schindler never shrank from facing high risks on their behalf. Rena Finder, a *Schindlerjude*, remarked that the fast-talking Schindler loved flirting with danger. "I think he was a gambler and loved to outwit the SS. In the beginning, it was a game. It was fun at first. He joined the [Nazi Party] to make money. But he had no stomach for the killing. He enjoyed the wheeling and dealing and doing outrageous things—living on the edge. But then he realized if he didn't save us, nobody would."[45]

Schindler succeeded, in part, because he was no saint. He freely associated with Nazis and, in a way, shared many of the same traits as the men he grew to despise. He beat the Nazis because he knew their system and understood their style. As war's end drew near, however, Schindler would find the tables reversed. The Nazi system was about to collapse in ruins, and with it Schindler's world.

Chapter Six

"As If He Had Saved the Whole World"

Since 1939, Schindler had been able to concentrate on running his factory and protecting his workers. That changed in late April 1945, when it became apparent that the Russian army would soon arrive in the Brinnlitz region. Now, rather than Schindler being the provider, he became the one in need of help. The *Schindlerjuden* were more than willing to repay his kindness with that of their own.

"We Started to Cry and Kiss Each Other"

In the final week of April, Schindler learned of a telegram from the commandant of Gross Rosen to another official in Brinnlitz that covered the steps to be taken in eliminating Schindler's Jews once the Russian army appeared. The memo stated that the aged and ill would be immediately shot and the healthy taken to the Mauthausen death camp. Schindler once more used his influence with high Nazi administrators to have the Brinnlitz official replaced with another who was more friendly, but he knew that he would soon be unable to shield his people. Already, rumors swirled about the barracks of Polish laborers digging huge mass graves in the forests near Brinnlitz to dispose of the Jews.

Schindler had even more on his mind. As German soldiers retreated from the Russian army toward Germany, they would more frequently pass by the factory. Schindler wondered if they would decide to vent their rage on helpless Jews inside Brinnlitz. He also feared what the Russians would do to him and Emilie should they capture the couple.

He had heard rumors that the Russians immediately executed any German civilians they captured.

To defend his workers and his wife, Schindler had accumulated a small collection of weapons and stored them in a room next to his office. He gave the key to a worker and ordered him to hand out the rifles, pistols, and hand grenades should the Nazi guards at Brinnlitz try to slaughter them. Another Jew who had been an officer in the Polish army, Uri Bejski, trained fifteen workers on how to use the weapons.

On May 7, 1945, Schindler learned from a British radio broadcast that the war would officially end at midnight on May 8. Bronia Gunz, a *Schindler-jude*, said that for the first time she experienced something she had not heard in years—silence. "It was so quiet. I said, 'Something is happening here.' We didn't see guards. Schindler said that the war was over. Slowly, we started to put our heads out from the barracks. We started to cry and kiss each other."[46] Schindler arranged to have British prime minister Winston Churchill's victory speech piped through loudspeakers at the factory.

The news set Bejski and his fifteen men in motion. They grabbed the weapons from Schindler's storage room and took positions around the factory, prepared to fight any Nazi guards that might enter with the intent to murder

The Death of Hitler

The man most responsible for causing the Holocaust, Adolf Hitler, helped bring about its end with his own death. As the Soviet, American, and British armies closed in on Germany from both the western and eastern fronts, Hitler governed a rapidly dwindling country. Now ruling from a fortifed Berlin bunker burrowed deep in the ground, Hitler realized as April 1945 closed that defeat was inevitable.

Instead of facing capture and standing trial for his deeds, Hitler opted for another way out. On April 30, he and longtime mistress Eva Braun entered a room in the bunker, where Braun swallowed poison and Hitler shot himself in the head. A handful of officers then carried the bodies to the courtyard above the bunker, soaked the bodies in gasoline, and set them on fire.

The war officially ended soon after, and concentration camp victims were finally free to rebuild their lives. A horrible era, a time that visited death and suffering upon millions of people, had finally ceased.

Prisoners at Dachau concentration camp cheer the American troops who liberated the camp on May 3, 1945.

people. Poldek Pfefferberg and another man disarmed the commanding officer. The other guards—too old to fight and reluctant to give their lives in what was now a lost cause—willingly handed over their rifles. By midnight on May 8, most guards had fled the area.

For some time Schindler had been amassing eighteen truckloads of shoes, uniforms, and coat fabric. The material was supposedly intended for a govern-

ment agency for which Schindler had agreed to store the items. He now opened the supply room and handed out $150,000 worth of supplies. Each worker received three yards of cotton cloth from which to sew new clothes, a complete set of underwear, two hundred cigarettes, and a bottle of vodka they could use to barter for more valuable products. Schindler hoped these gifts would enable his people to begin reconstructing their lives now that the war had ended.

"The [Words] That Had to Be Said"

Schindler hurriedly set in motion the steps he had planned for his departure. In an emotional incident recorded by Thomas Keneally in his book *Schindler's List*, Schindler spoke to his workers, who quietly gathered together to hear his words. Two women who knew shorthand scribbled down what their benefactor muttered. He began by asking for restraint:

> The unconditional surrender of Germany has just been announced. After six years of the cruel murder of human beings, victims are being mourned, and Europe is now trying to return to peace and order. I would like to turn to you for unconditional order and discipline—to all of you who together with me have

worried through many hard years—in order that you can live through the present and within a few days go back to your destroyed and plundered homes, looking for survivors from your families. You will thus prevent panic, whose results cannot be foreseen.

He next said words that must have been difficult for his Jewish laborers to hear—that all Germans should not be blamed for the actions of a few deranged murderers, and that they should avoid seeking vengeance through violence. "If you have to accuse a person, do it in the right place. Because in the new Europe there will be judges, incorruptible judges, who will listen to you." Schindler, with his voice growing weary and breaking with passion, pledged to continue helping as long as he could. "I have done everything and spent most every effort in getting you additional food, and I pledge to do the utmost in the future to protect

Revenge

Following Schindler's departure from the Brinnlitz factory in May 1945, some of the younger Jewish workers vented their anger. They grabbed one guard who had been particularly harsh, dragged him to the factory hall, and hanged him from a beam. Other Jews tried to prevent it, arguing that such an action made them no better than their Nazi tormentors, but they could not dissuade their cohorts. Though most *Schindlerjuden* listened to Schindler's words promoting decent behavior, a few had apparently experienced too much for them to remain passive.

you and safeguard your daily bread."[47] He promised to remain at Brinnlitz until after the final Nazi guards had fled, then asked for three minutes of silence for those who did not survive the war. With these final words, he and Emilie headed to their apartment to pack for a difficult journey.

Some accounts of the final moments at Brinnlitz claim that Schindler never delivered the speech, but Emilie says they are incorrect. In her memoirs, she writes, "Those were his words, the ones that had to be said at a moment like this. I felt very proud to be there, at his side."[48]

Schindler in Flight

Schindler now entered the part of his life where roles reversed. Instead of providing assistance to his workers and keeping them alive, he now needed them. He had to turn to his Jews for aid and shelter. Dressed in the same striped uniforms worn by Itzhak Stern and the other Jews, he and Emilie packed their belongings in Schindler's Mercedes Benz and joined eight workers who had volunteered to accompany the couple. A truck, jammed with commodities for barter, sat behind the Mercedes.

Before Schindler stepped into the vehicle, now surrounded by people anxious to bid farewell, a delegation of workers handed him a letter written in Hebrew that explained all that he had done for the Jews at Emalia and Brinnlitz. They hoped that in his flight toward the west, Schindler would encounter a unit of American soldiers, which often contained a rabbi for religious purposes. If the Americans understood Schindler's contributions, they might not incarcerate him with suspected Nazis.

While two workers carefully tore open the upholstery in Schindler's Mercedes and hid small bags of diamonds inside the car's frame, other workers presented a beautiful gift to Schindler—a ring made from the gold teeth of a man named Jeret. Inscribed on the ring's interior was a verse from the Talmud, a Jewish sacred book: "Whoever saves a single soul, it is as if he had saved the whole world."[49]

Oskar and Emilie then stepped into the car to leave. Emilie wrote years later, "I will never forget the expression on their faces, a mixture of sadness, gratitude, and hope. Nor will I ever forget their gesture of preparing a document for us, a kind of diploma, drawn on whatever pieces of paper they could find, and which most of them had signed, testifying to what we had done for them."[50]

The Schindlers had little time to waste, since the Russian army was expected at any moment. If he were captured by the Soviets, Schindler might instantly be executed as a Nazi. When the driver of his vehicle tried to start the car, the engine refused to turn over. Poldek Pfefferberg hastily checked

Allied guards march a group of German POWs through a German town at the end of the war. As Schindler fled to the west, he feared being taken into custody as a suspected Nazi.

underneath the hood and discovered a severed wire, and as Schindler anxiously checked for signs of the Russians, Pfefferberg repaired the problem.

As Schindler's car drove off, the Jewish workers, many with tears coursing down their cheeks, stared at the man who had been their provider for so many years. They had always counted on him in times of crisis, but now they were left alone. Instead of remembering the strong, affable man, their final image of Schindler was of a man in flight to save his life. The *Schindlerjuden* were free, but they faced a future fraught with fear and uncertainty. Betty Sternlicht recalled that "We were holding one another. He was our father."[51]

The Schindlers and the eight former workers headed southwest toward Switzerland because one of the workers had relatives in the country. Czech underground fighters halted the vehicles that first night and directed Schindler's party to the nearby town of Havlickuv Brod, where Red Cross officials suggested they spend the night in the safest place—the jail.

A surprise awaited them the next morning. Overnight, unknown individuals had stripped both vehicles, removed all valuables, including the bags of diamonds, and even stolen the tires. As a result, the ten refugees traveled by train south toward the Swiss border as far as it would go, then got out and walked through the forests.

They finally encountered a group of American soldiers near the Czech village of Eleanorenhain. The unit, led by intelligence officer Kurt Klein, took the refugees into custody just like they would have done to any other people wandering in the forest. As Klein explained,

> Nobody knew who he was at the time. They were all dressed in prison uniforms and presented themselves as refugees from a German labor camp. They didn't let on that Schindler, their Nazi labor camp director, was in their midst, probably because they were afraid I would arrest him as a POW [prisoner of war]. They were correct, because my assignment was to interrogate and segregate Germans caught fleeing from the Russian and Czech guns.[52]

Fortunately, Klein's squad included a rabbi who understood enough Hebrew to read the letter handed to him by Schindler. The rabbi broke down in tears as he told the other American soldiers about what Schindler had done. Klein immediately arranged for food and a place for the group to stay for two days. The rabbi obtained a vehicle for the Schindler party's use, but the group was halted again at Linz in upper Austria, where American soldiers took them to a holding center. When the Jews in Schindler's group told the interrogators of their incredible experiences and how Schindler had saved them, the Americans placed them in a lakeside hotel until the proper paperwork could be completed and they could be let go.

"To Begin His Life Anew"

Now penniless because they had lost everything of value during their flight, Oskar and Emilie lived for a few months with two Jews they had helped at Plaszow—Henry and Leopold Rosner. Schindler, bedecked in a tattered overcoat, had nothing waiting for him in either Krakow or Moravia, since the Russians had confiscated all his property and the immense fortune he had accumulated during the war years had been spent assisting his Jewish workers. The few items of jewelry not stolen from his stripped Mercedes had long been bartered away for food.

In the latter years of the 1940s, the couple lived in Regensburg and Munich, Germany, relying on packages of food and clothing from American and Polish relief organizations to survive. Whenever he was asked for assistance by American legal authorities collecting evidence of war crimes, which frequently occurred, Schindler provided information on the

Bigotry Goes On

Bigotry and hatred share equal billing for causing the Holocaust. Though the era occurred more than half a century ago, the bitter emotions remain to poison relationships among people. Even during the filming of the movie *Schindler's List*, an incident that occurred showed that bigotry is never far from the surface. Writer Frank Sanello included the episode in his biography *Spielberg*.

As Sanello explains, actor Ben Kingsley, who played Itzhak Stern, shared drinks with a Jewish actor one night in a German tavern. As the two talked, a German businessman walked up and asked the actor with Kingsley if he was a Jew. When the man replied that he was, the businessman drew an imaginary noose with his hand and said, "Hitler should have finished the job." Kingsley had to be restrained by other actors from assaulting the offending individual.

Actor Ben Kingsley (center) portrays Itzhak Stern in a scene from *Schindler's List*.

Nazi officials stand trial for their crimes at the International Military Tribunal in Nuremberg. Schindler often provided assistance to postwar authorities collecting evidence of war crimes.

Nazi officials with whom he had worked. For instance, Amon Goeth was found guilty of crimes against humanity and hanged in Krakow on September 13, 1946. Because of his cooperation and his life-saving efforts for his Jews during the war, Schindler became the target of abuse by some German citizens. Businessmen shunned him and pedestrians occasionally hurled rocks in his direction, but Schindler carried on.

In October 1945 he had applied for help from the United Nations Relief and Rehabilitation Administration, a charitable organization established to assist people who lost most of their belongings in the war. But he had to overcome a dubious official before receiving anything. When Schindler produced a copy of his famous list to support his story, the official relented and approved Schindler's request.

In 1949, Schindler joined many of the *Schindlerjuden* for a festive reunion in Paris, France. The men and women he had saved noticed his tattered clothes and realized the extent of his impoverishment. Later that year, an international Jewish relief organization called the Joint Distribution Committee handed Schindler $15,000 and a letter of reference in an attempt to repay the

A group of *Schindlerjuden* at a 1949 reunion in Paris pays tribute to the man who saved their lives.

businessman for what he had done. The letter stated that the organization "has thoroughly investigated the wartime and Occupation activities of Mr. Schindler. We recommend wholeheartedly that all organizations and individuals contacted by Mr. Schindler do their utmost to help him, in recognition of his outstanding service." The letter went on to explain that

> Under the guise of operating a Nazi labor factory first in Poland [Emalia] and then in the Sudetenland [Brinnlitz], Mr. Schindler

managed to take in as employees and protect Jewish men and women destined for death in Auschwitz or other infamous concentration camps. "Schindler's camp in Brinnlitz," witnesses have told the Joint Distribution Committee, "was the only camp in the Nazi-occupied territories where a Jew was never killed, or even beaten, but was always treated as a human being."

The lengthy letter ended with a plea to the reader to open his heart as Schindler had once done for the Jews.

"Now that he is about to begin his life anew, let us help him as once he helped our brethren."[53]

As always, Schindler kept the news of his money from Emilie. She never saw a penny. Her husband wasted it on luxuries and women while Emilie scoured the black market to place food on the table. Although she often considered leaving Oskar, Emilie always remained because of her religion and what divorce might do to her parents. "I had no choice but to adapt," she claimed, "to tighten my lips and close my eyes to Oskar's neglect and indifference. I shed many bitter tears because of him, but in time I toughened up."[54]

Emilie had more travails to face with her husband, who now saw opportunities outside of Germany. He thought that if he could not succeed and find happiness in his homeland, maybe in another land he could once again regain the success he had in wartime Europe. In 1949 Oskar and Emilie crossed the Atlantic Ocean to start over on a new continent.

Chapter Seven

"AN ORDINARY MAN . . . AND YET HE DID IT"

In October 1949 Oskar and Emilie Schindler boarded a passenger liner bound for Argentina, a nation along the eastern coast of South America with a considerable German and Jewish population. Schindler hoped that, away from the bitterness and memories that engulfed him in Germany, he might be able to fashion a decent life in a new land. The man who had found happiness and adventure during the war, however, would find neither in Argentina. It took a powerful book and an even more compelling movie to restore Schindler's reputation.

"Eager to Go Somewhere Else"

Although by now it probably was not much of a surprise to Emilie, Oskar also brought to Argentina his current mistress, a girl named Gisa. Emilie did not object, believing her words would fall on deaf ears and would only aggravate the situation. As she wrote in her memoirs, she also "did not have the energy for futile reproaches anymore."[55] In time, the two women became friends.

The three arrived in Argentina's capital, Buenos Aires, on November 3, 1949. Emilie quickly fell in love with the sprawling city, but Oskar walked around as if in a trance. His energy level, usually maintained at heights most individuals would find tiring, failed to reappear. "Everything communicated a happy and positive feeling," wrote Emilie, "except for Oskar's face, which seemed to say that he was watching a movie he had no interest in seeing, and was eager to go somewhere else."[56] Schindler loved a fast-paced world, whether it be in motorcycle racing or in outmaneuvering Nazi officials, and Argentina seemed tame by comparison.

The couple—Gisa lived in her own place—established a farm raising fur-bearing animals called nutria. However, because Oskar constantly traveled about the country establishing business contacts, Emilie had to take charge of the company. Within a few years, mainly due to lack of interest on Schindler's part, the business went bankrupt and he and Emilie moved into a home near Buenos Aires provided by his Jewish supporters. He accepted a job as a sales representa-

tive, but gave it up in less than a year when he found no satisfaction in it.

In 1957 Schindler learned that the German government had agreed to compensate those who had suffered financially under the Nazi tyranny. Leaving Emilie and Gisa behind so that he would be free to pursue his own interests, Schindler returned to Germany to establish the value of his business, received a large sum of money, and then remained in Europe without ever seeing his wife again. He moved into a small Frankfurt apartment, and quickly spent the money on various projects that eventually failed.

In 1949 Schindler moved with his wife and mistress to the bustling city of Buenos Aires, Argentina.

Nothing he tried, including a cement factory, succeeded. It seemed that the man who supervised a thriving industry during wartime could do nothing right in calmer times. He loved competing when it entailed bribery, exciting challenges, and fast deals with dangerous people, but now all that had been taken away. A news reporter who interviewed Schindler claimed that "It turned out in the end that Oskar Schindler was a salesman, a dreamer—and a very bad honest businessman."[57]

Moshe Bejski and other *Schindlerjuden* provided financial assistance to Schindler during this time, but nothing seemed to remedy the situation. Bejski later said, "After the war, he was quite unable to run a normal business. During the war, as long as he could produce kitchenware and sell it on the black market and make a lot of money, he could do it. But he was unable to work normally, to calculate normally, to hold down a normal job, even in Germany. A group of survivors in Israel raised some money for him when he was hard up. If we sent $3,000–$4,000, he spent it within two or three weeks, then phoned to say he didn't have a penny. He spent money quicker than we could raise it."[58] In the early 1960s a movie studio paid Schindler $20,000 for the rights to film his story (the movie was never made), and the money was gone within one week. Alcohol, fine clothes, and fast living continued to be more important to Schindler than saving money.

Schindler received a mixed reaction in Germany. Hoping to shed its wartime image, in 1966 the German government awarded Schindler the Cross of Merit, one of the country's highest honors. Two years later, the German Ministry of Finance agreed to pay him a small monthly pension as compensation for his wartime losses. A German television station aired Schindler's story.

At the same time, Schindler served as an unwelcome reminder to some German citizens of an era they wanted

Schindler struggled financially and emotionally following the war.

to forget, a time when many people turned a blind eye toward the Nazi evil. Cries of "Jew lover" and other phrases meant as insults sometimes greeted Schindler as he walked around town. In 1963 Schindler had to appear in a German court after punching a man who called him a "Jew kisser." The judge, instead of admonishing the insulter, scolded Schindler for the physical assault and ordered him to pay damages to the man. A dejected Schindler wrote to his friend Henry Rosner, who now lived in New York, "I would kill myself if it wouldn't give them so much satisfaction."[59]

Help from His Jews

Once again, Schindler's people came through for him when he most needed it. After learning of his despair, plus hearing that his cement factory had gone bankrupt, in 1961 the *Schindlerjuden* in Israel invited Schindler to Tel Aviv to honor him. On his fifty-third birthday, the state of Israel unveiled a plaque in his honor in the city's Park of Heroes, a spot set aside to memorialize individuals of conscience and courage. Ten days later, Israel declared Schindler a "righteous Gentile" deserving of every Jew's honor. State authorities planted a tree bearing Schindler's name along the Avenue of the Righteous leading to the prominent Yad Vashem museum, the depository of important Jewish historical and political records.

Schindler stands in front of a tree planted in his honor at Yad Vashem, the Israeli Holocaust memorial museum in Jerusalem.

A moved Schindler so enjoyed the festivities and reception that he returned to Israel every year to celebrate his birthday. When he lacked funds to finance the voyage, as he usually did, the *Schindlerjuden* supplied the money. The family that Schindler lacked as a child, had ignored as an adult, and had longed for all his life had now been found.

The *Schindlerjuden* helped in other ways as well. From his home in Los Angeles, Poldek Pfefferberg wrote other Jews and urged them to contribute one day's pay each year to support Oskar Schindler. In 1968

Pfefferberg established a foundation to supervise the money and ensure that Schindler could live in relative comfort for the rest of his life. Four years later, another *Schindlerjude*, Murray Pantirer, raised $120,000 to fund a floor dedicated to Schindler at the Truman Research Center at Hebrew University in Tel Aviv.

"Oskar's Last Flirtation"

Schindler lived in this manner until October 9, 1974, when he collapsed in his small Frankfurt apartment and died. Controversy has arisen over the cause of his death. The official death certificate lists hardening of the arteries as the principal factor, and Emilie was told that a heart attack killed her husband. She wrote in her memoirs, though, that she learned during a 1995 trip to Germany that Oskar died on the operating table during a procedure to replace his heart pacemaker. According to her sources, suspicion of foul play circulated because of rumors that Schindler had had an affair with the wife of the surgeon performing the procedure. Emilie labeled it "Oskar's last flirtation with danger."[60]

At Schindler's request, he was buried in the Latin Cemetery, a Catholic burial ground in Jerusalem, so that he could be near the people he had shielded during the war. A huge crowd, including many of his *Schindlerjuden*, gathered in Jerusalem for the funeral procession, which meandered through the city's

Emilie Schindler (pictured in 1993) was neglected and eventually abandoned by her husband in 1957.

streets before finishing at the cemetery. On his tombstone, an inscription read, "The unforgettable savior of 1,200 Jews."

What happened to Emilie? As of this writing she still lives in Argentina in the home purchased for her by a Jewish organization, B'nai B'rith. A small pension helps her live decently, and a flood of letters provides the warmth and love that Oskar never could deliver.

A Remarkable Book, a Powerful Movie

Six years after Schindler died, author Thomas Keneally stopped in a Beverly

Hills, California, luggage shop during a book promotion tour. While there he met the shop's owner, Poldek Pfefferberg, who started telling Keneally about Oskar Schindler. Pfefferberg had spent years trying to interest a writer in the story, and the more Pfefferberg talked, the more convinced Keneally became that this was a special story.

The story eventually became a best-selling novel, which brought Oskar Schindler into the lives of readers around the world. *Schindler's Ark* (later renamed *Schindler's List*) garnered numerous awards when it appeared in 1982, including Britain's Booker Prize for fiction (though based on facts, it was technically a work of fiction since many of the conversations had not been recorded and had to be re-created). One of those who read it, noted Hollywood director Steven Spielberg, was so moved that he decided to turn

Author Thomas Keneally (pictured) wrote his best-selling 1982 novel *Schindler's Ark* after talking with *Schindlerjude* Poldek Pfefferberg during a chance meeting.

Schindler's Ark into a movie. Spielberg, himself a Jew, had noticed the rise of hatred in different parts of the world and believed that a movie depicting one man battling bigotry might convey an appropriate message. As Spielberg stated,

> There was CNN reporting every day on the equivalent to the Nazi death camps in Bosnia, the atrocities against the Muslims—and then this horrible word "ethnic cleansing," cousin to the "final solution." I thought, "My God, this is happening again." And on top of all that comes the media giving serious air time and print space to the Holocaust deniers, the people who claim that the Holocaust never happened, that six million weren't killed, that it's all some kind of hoax.[61]

Spielberg visited Auschwitz before the start of filming. He expected to be affected by what he saw, but the intense anger that burned inside him as he walked about the immense death camp surprised him. "I felt so helpless, that there was nothing I could do about it. And yet I thought, well, there is something I can do about it. I can make *Schindler's List*. I mean, it's not going to bring anybody back alive, but it maybe will remind people that another Holocaust is a sad possibility."[62]

Ironically, when Spielberg headed to Poland to film the movie, he could not find enough Jewish actors to portray the numerous roles required in the film. Spielberg wanted to use Jewish actors for realism, but he "couldn't find any Jews in Poland to be the Jews in the movie because Hitler had murdered them all."[63]

Spielberg, who later donated $50,000 to wipe out Emilie's debts,

Making the Movie

Steven Spielberg had difficulty getting the movie *Schindler's List* started. He first had to convince Hollywood backers that such a film would be profitable. He did so by appealing to Schindler's conflicting characteristics. As he explained in Joseph McBride's *Steven Spielberg: A Biography*, "I was drawn to [the project] because of the paradoxical nature of the character. It wasn't about a Jew saving Jews, or a neutral person from Sweden or Switzerland saving Jews. It was about a Nazi saving Jews. What would drive a man like this to suddenly take everything he had earned and put it all in the service of saving these lives?"

Steven Spielberg directs Liam Neeson in his Academy Award–winning film *Schindler's List,* an adaptation of Keneally's moving novel.

flew Oskar's wife to Jerusalem when he filmed the movie's final scene, which depicts a gathering of *Schindlerjuden* at Oskar's grave. Emilie was later asked if Oskar was as handsome as Liam Neeson, the actor who portrayed her husband. She replied that Neeson certainly made an impression on her, but he could not surpass the impact her husband had: "I smiled [at the question], thinking of his elegant bearing, handsome looks, blond hair, lively and intensely blue eyes, plus a smile that became quite seductive unintentionally,

and I knew that again, I would choose Oskar."[64]

Spielberg's 1993 movie exceeded all expectations by grossing more than $320 million worldwide. Schools throughout the United States aired the movie for students, and the film swept most top industry honors. The Los Angeles Film Critics Association, the New York Film Critics Circle, and the National Board of Review all named *Schindler's List* the best film of 1993, and the movie earned seven Academy Awards, including Oscars for Best Picture and Best Director.

Help from a Friend

Filming the movie about Oskar Schindler proved to be the most difficult experience of Steven Spielberg's professional life. Particularly arduous were the scenes involving Amon Goeth at Plaszow and the elimination of the Krakow ghetto, both of which almost sickened the filmmaker. After working on the scenes for days at a time, Spielberg found that he needed relief from the depression and anger he felt. He turned to an old friend for help. In his book *Oskar Schindler and His List,* author Thomas Fensch quotes Spielberg as saying that "every single day was like waking up and going to hell, really. There were no jokes on the set. No funny outtakes to show at the wrap party. Twice in the production I called [comedian] Robin Williams just to say, Robin, I haven't laughed in seven weeks. Help me here. And Robin would do twenty minutes [of comedy] on the telephone."

Frightened Jews are loaded onto boxcars in this harrowing scene from the movie.

Schindler's Legacy

The movie focused the world spotlight on Schindler's name and actions and helped ensure that Schindler's legacy continues. The businessman impacted people during the war as well as after it. He saved more than one thousand people, most of whom later moved on to productive careers and families. Sons and daughters were born that would never have been, marriages and occupations established that would not have been formed. One *Schindlerjude* stated that "Thanks to Schindler's efforts, we survived as a family. My wife and myself have parents, and my children have grandparents."[65]

Schindler influenced people he never met. Steven Spielberg was so moved by his story that in 1994 he established the Shoah Visual History Foundation to videotape the recollec-

tions of fifty thousand survivors of the Holocaust. So many Jews approached Spielberg with their stories after the movie arrived in theaters that he realized he had another duty—to record their tales before they died. According to Spielberg, many of the survivors asked him, "Will you take my testimony? Can I, before I die, tell somebody—tell you, with a camera—what happened to me, so my children will know, so my friends will finally know, and so I can leave something of myself behind so the world will know."[66] Spielberg became convinced that this was the true reason he had made the movie.

The *Schindlerjuden* who are still alive feel a responsibility to tell the world about hatred and to counter the arguments cast by those, mainly neo-Nazis who espouse Hitler's views, who defend Hitler as a great man and contend that

Street Names

Oskar Schindler lives on in many ways. Thomas Keneally's book and Steven Spielberg's movie ensure that future generations will know his story, but in smaller ways his legacy continues. Murray Pantirer, a *Schindlerjude*, fashioned a prosperous career constructing homes in the eastern United States. Each time he started a new project, he made sure that Schindler became a part of it by naming one of the streets Schindler Drive. As he explained in Elinor J. Brecher's *Schindler's Legacy*, "Right now, in almost twenty towns in New Jersey and Pennsylvania, we have Schindler Drives. Our children in business with us know that whenever they build in a new town, they must name at least one street after Schindler."

the Holocaust never happened. They would not have had this opportunity if Schindler had not saved their lives, so they honor his memory by speaking out. Rena Ferber Finder never before mentioned her experiences in public, but now that some deny the Holocaust's existence, she feels obligated to take action: "We realized we had to say something. Time was growing short, and people were dying. I feel it is my duty to talk."[67] Through Finder's words and the utterances of other *Schindlerjuden*, Schindler continues to battle prejudice in death just as he did in life.

Helen Sternlicht puts it as powerfully:

> It was meant for me to speak for all the people that perished. This is one of the reasons I put myself out to speak so much. For me, this is the most important thing. My neighbors say, "Helen, we are so proud of you. We are cutting out everything about you from the newspapers and we give them to our children and make them promise to give them to their children." It is so meaningful to me that people want to know and tell their kids.[68]

Above all, the story of Oskar Schindler shows that an individual can make a difference. In an era when thousands of people, inside and outside Germany, claimed they could do noth-

Schindler stands next to the Jewish Holocaust Memorial in Germany.

ing to stop evil, he stood up and took action. Schindler was one against many, the decent person recognizing evil and doing what he could to oppose it. Leon Leyson, a *Schindlerjude*, explained it this way: "Each one of us at any time, faced with the particular circumstances, has the power to stand on the side of right. Ninety-nine percent of the time, we simply don't. This is an ordinary man, not a special hero with super powers, and yet he did it."[69]

That is what makes Schindler so remarkable—that he was an ordinary human being fraught with shortcomings like most people yet he took a stand against evil. Sol Urbach, a *Schindlerjude*, claimed that those who deny the Holocaust ever happened did not worry him as much as the rest of the population, for from personal experience he knew that most people confronted by evil remain silent. "When hate groups spring up, those who stand by and don't do anything are really helping spread the hate,"[70] Urbach claimed.

Oskar Schindler did something, and in his actions showed the world that one person can make a difference. This lesson may be his greatest legacy.

NOTES

Introduction: "We Only Did What We Had To"

1. Emilie Schindler, with Erika Rosenberg, *Where Light and Shadow Meet: A Memoir.* New York: W.W. Norton, 1996, p. ix.

Chapter One: Acting to the Circumstances

2. Schindler, *Where Light and Shadow Meet*, p. 24.
3. Quoted in Schindler, *Where Light and Shadow Meet*, p. 25.
4. Schindler, *Where Light and Shadow Meet*, p. 28.
5. Schindler, *Where Light and Shadow Meet*, p. 37.

Chapter Two: "I'm Gonna Make a Lot of Money"

6. Quoted on *A&E Biography*, "Oskar Schindler: The Man Behind the List," 1998.
7. Quoted in Thomas Fensch, ed., *Oskar Schindler and His List.* Forest Dale, VT: Paul S. Eriksson, 1995, p. 22.
8. Quoted in Elinor J. Brecher, *Schindler's Legacy.* New York: Dutton, 1994, p. 18.

9. Quoted in Thomas Keneally, *Schindler's List.* New York: Simon and Schuster, 1982, p. 74.
10. Quoted in Fensch, *Oskar Schindler and His List*, p. 26.
11. Quoted in Keneally, *Schindler's List*, p. 91.

Chapter Three: "Everything in My Power"

12. Quoted in Keneally, *Schindler's List*, pp. 124–25.
13. Quoted in Keneally, *Schindler's List*, p. 133.
14. Keneally, *Schindler's List*, p. 171.
15. Schindler, *Where Light and Shadow Meet*, p. 59.
16. Quoted in Brecher, *Schindler's Legacy*, p. 62.
17. Quoted in Brecher, *Schindler's Legacy*, p. 62.
18. Quoted in Brecher, *Schindler's Legacy*, p. 64.

Chapter Four: "Who Works for Me, Lives"

19. Schindler, *Where Light and Shadow Meet*, p. 46.
20. Keneally, *Schindler's List*, p. 202.
21. Quoted in Fensch, *Oskar Schindler*

and His List, p. 25.

22. Quoted in Eric Silver, *The Book of the Just: The Unsung Heroes Who Rescued Jews from Hitler.* New York: Grove Press, 1992, p. 149.

23. Quoted in Brecher, *Schindler's Legacy*, p. 151.

24. Quoted in Brecher, *Schindler's Legacy*, p. 180.

25. Quoted in Brecher, *Schindler's Legacy*, p. xviii.

26. Quoted in Silver, *The Book of the Just*, p. 149.

27. Quoted on *A&E Biography*, "Oskar Schindler."

28. Quoted in Brecher, *Schindler's Legacy*, p. 385.

29. Quoted in Brecher, *Schindler's Legacy*, p. 384.

30. Quoted in Brecher, *Schindler's Legacy*, p. 363.

31. Quoted in Joseph McBride, *Steven Spielberg: A Biography.* New York: Simon and Schuster, 1997, p. 439.

32. Quoted in Silver, *The Book of the Just*, pp. 147–48.

33. Quoted in McBride, *Steven Spielberg*, p. 439.

34. Quoted in Keneally, *Schindler's List*, p. 252.

Chapter Five: "You're with Me Now"

35. Quoted in Brecher, *Schindler's Legacy*, p. 321.

36. Quoted in Silver, *The Book of the Just*, p. 151.

37. Quoted in Brecher, *Schindler's Legacy*, p. xxx.

38. Quoted in Brecher, *Schindler's Legacy*, p. 14.

39. Quoted in Keneally, *Schindler's List*, p. 319.

40. Quoted in Keneally, *Schindler's List*, p. 330.

41. Quoted in Milton Meltzer, *Rescue: The Story of How Gentiles Saved Jews in the Holocaust.* New York: Harper and Row, 1988, p. 66.

42. Keneally, *Schindler's List*, p. 336.

43. Quoted in Keneally, *Schindler's List*, p. 333.

44. Quoted in Schindler, *Where Light and Shadow Meet*, p. 89.

45. Quoted in Brecher, *Schindler's Legacy*, p. xxxii.

Chapter Six: "As If He Had Saved the Whole World"

46. Quoted in Brecher, *Schindler's Legacy*, p. 363.

47. Quoted in Keneally, *Schindler's List*, pp. 369–71.

48. Schindler, *Where Light and Shadow Meet*, p. 96.

49. Quoted in Meltzer, *Rescue*, p. 67.

50. Schindler, *Where Light and Shadow Meet*, p. 101.

51. Quoted in Brecher, *Schindler's Legacy*, p. 70.

52. Quoted in Brecher, *Schindler's Legacy*, p. xxxvi.

53. Quoted in Keneally, *Schindler's List*, p. 391.

54. Schindler, *Where Light and Shadow Meet*, pp. 117–18.

Chapter Seven: "An Ordinary Man . . . and Yet He Did It"

55. Schindler, *Where Light and Shadow Meet*, p. 131.

56. Schindler, *Where Light and Shadow Meet*, p. 125.

57. Quoted in Fensch, *Oskar Schindler and His List*, p. 18.

58. Quoted in Silver, *The Book of the Just*, pp. 147–48.

59. Quoted in Keneally, *Schindler's List*, p. 394.

60. Schindler, *Where Light and Shadow Meet*, p. 145.

61. Quoted in McBride, *Steven Spielberg*, p. 427.

62. Quoted in Fensch, *Oskar Schindler and His List*, p. 61.

63. Quoted in Fensch, *Oskar Schindler and His List*, p. 61.

64. Schindler, *Where Light and Shadow Meet*, p. 128.

65. Quoted on *A&E Biography*, "Oskar Schindler."

66. Quoted in McBride, *Steven Spielberg*, pp. 442–43.

67. Quoted in Brecher, *Schindler's Legacy*, p. 156.

68. Quoted in Brecher, *Schindler's Legacy*, p. 76.

69. Quoted in Brecher, *Schindler's Legacy*, p. xxxvii.

70. Quoted in Brecher, *Schindler's Legacy*, p. 254.

FOR FURTHER READING

David A. Adler, *We Remember the Holocaust.* New York: Henry Holt, 1989. A superb account of the Holocaust for young readers, based heavily on personal recollections.

Richard Amdur, *Anne Frank.* New York: Chelsea House, 1993. An excellent biography intended for the teenage market.

Susan D. Bachrach, *Tell Them We Remember: The Story of the Holocaust.* Boston: Little, Brown, 1994. Printed in conjunction with the U.S. Holocaust Memorial Museum, this book supplements informative text with numerous photographs.

Gay Block and Malka Drucker, *Rescuers: Portraits of Moral Courage in the Holocaust.* New York: Holmes and Meier, 1992. This is a superb book for learning about other non-Jews who saved Jews from the Holocaust. The authors profile 105 rescuers from ten nations.

Jacob Boas, *We Are Witnesses: Five Diaries of Teenagers Who Died in the Holocaust.* New York: Scholastic, 1995. Gripping accounts of life during the Holocaust, written by five Jewish teenagers who died in the war.

Janrense Boonstra and Marie-José Rijnders, *Anne Frank House.* Amsterdam: Sdu Uitgeverij Koninginnegracht, 1992. Informative book about the Anne Frank Museum and the life and times of Anne Frank.

Alison Leslie Gold, *Memories of Anne Frank: Reflections of a Childhood Friend.* New York: Scholastic, 1997. A powerful book that contains remembrances of Anne Frank by individuals who knew her.

Laurel Holliday, *Why Do They Hate Me?* New York: Pocket Books, 1999. This collection of diaries, written by young people involved in the Holocaust, provides a powerful account of what life was like for young Jews during that horrible time.

Michael Leapman, *Witness to War: Eight True-Life Stories of Nazi Persecution.* New York: Scholastic, 1998. Leapman's book, written in narrative form and detailing the lives of young people caught in the

Holocaust, is a solid complement to Holliday's collection.

Willy Lindwer, *The Last Seven Months of Anne Frank*. New York: Anchor Books, 1991. Survivors of the Holocaust, each of whom knew Anne Frank or were incarcerated in the same concentration camps as Anne, provide stirring accounts of the young woman.

Milton Meltzer, *Never to Forget: The Jews of the Holocaust*. New York: Harper and Row, 1976. Useful recounting for younger readers of the Holocaust's impact.

Abraham Resnick, *The Holocaust*. San Diego: Lucent Books, 1991. A well-written history of the Holocaust for teenagers.

Jack L. Roberts, *The Importance of Oskar Schindler*. San Diego: Lucent Books, 1996. One of the few decent biographies of Schindler intended for the junior high/high school market. The volume contains valuable material about the Holocaust and life in the Krakow ghetto.

Michael A. Schuman, *Elie Wiesel: Voice from the Holocaust*. Hillside, NJ: Enslow, 1994. Excellent biography of a Holocaust survivor who became one of the most brilliant writers of our day.

Frank Dabba Smith, *My Secret Camera: Life in the Lodz Ghetto*. New York: Raintree/Steck Vaughn, 2000. A fine book about life in one of the worst ghettos of World War II.

Gail B. Stewart, *Hitler's Reich*. San Diego: Lucent Books, 1994. An informative account of life under Hitler's rule, written for the teenage market.

Helen Strahinich, *The Holocaust*. Springfield, NJ: Enslow, 1996. A basic history of the causes and effects of the Holocaust.

Ruud van der Rol and Rian Verhoeven, *Anne Frank: Beyond the Diary*. New York: Viking, 1993. A superb photobiography based on photographs and information supplied by the Anne Frank House and by Miep Gies.

Dennis Wepman, *Adolf Hitler*. New York: Chelsea House, 1985. An informative biography of the German leader for junior high school students.

WORKS CONSULTED

Books

Michael Berenbaum, *The World Must Know.* Boston: Little, Brown, 1993. Berenbaum's history of the Holocaust is one of the most informative, provocative accounts published. Many photographs supplement the text.

Elinor J. Brecher, *Schindler's Legacy.* New York: Dutton, 1994. The author interviewed more than forty *Schindlerjuden* to produce this moving book detailing the lives of some of the people Schindler saved. They unanimously attest to Schindler's decency, and credit him with giving them and their offspring a chance at life.

Lucy S. Dawidowicz, *The War Against the Jews: 1933–1945.* New York: Bantam Books, 1975. Scholarly account of the Holocaust by a prominent Holocaust historian.

Thomas Fensch, ed., *Oskar Schindler and His List.* Forest Dale, VT: Paul S. Eriksson, 1995. A very useful compilation of magazine and newspaper interviews and articles about Oskar Schindler, Steven Spielberg, and Spielberg's renowned movie. The first two are especially valuable—an interview with Herbert Steinhouse, a journalist who knew Schindler, and an article written by Steinhouse about Schindler's work.

Eva Fogelman, *Conscience and Courage: Rescuers of Jews During the Holocaust.* New York: Anchor Books, 1995. This book examines what motivated the Christians who helped save Jews in the war. It does not contain a great deal specifically on Schindler, but it helps the reader understand the personalities of men and women like him.

Martin Gilbert, *The Holocaust.* New York: Henry Holt, 1985. Gilbert delivers a readable survey of the Holocaust, including its origins, impact, and effects. Few one-volume histories of the Holocaust equal this one.

Daniel Jonah Goldhagen, *Hitler's Willing Executioners: Ordinary Germans and the Holocaust.* New York: Alfred A. Knopf, 1996. A thought-provoking book that examines the role of German citizens in the atrocities of these years.

Thomas Keneally, *Schindler's List.* New York: Simon and Schuster, 1982.

Even though the book is technically a work of fiction, since the author re-creates some conversations that were never recorded at the time, this is the most factual account existing of Oskar Schindler. Based on survivors' testimony, Keneally's book is the most important source for anyone researching Schindler.

Nora Levin, *The Holocaust: The Destruction of European Jewry, 1933–1945.* New York: Thomas Y. Crowell, 1968. A fine history of the Holocaust.

Joseph McBride, *Steven Spielberg: A Biography.* New York: Simon and Schuster, 1997. This superb biography of the talented movie director casts much light on Spielberg's decision to make *Schindler's List* and shows the impact the film made on him and others.

Milton Meltzer, *Rescue: The Story of How Gentiles Saved Jews in the Holocaust.* New York: Harper and Row, 1988. The author presents the stories of different individuals, including Schindler, who helped save Jewish lives throughout Europe. The chapter on Schindler is a good place to start researching his life.

Tadeusz Pankiewicz, *The Cracow Ghetto Pharmacy.* Washington, DC: Holocaust Library, 1947. Written by the owner of a pharmacy in Krakow during the war, this powerful book reveals more of what life was like for Jews in Krakow and Plaszow than it does about Oskar Schindler. The reader better understands the benefit of Schindler's work after finishing this volume.

Norman Polmar and Thomas B. Allen, *World War II: The Encyclopedia of the War Years, 1941–1945.* New York: Random House, 1996. Two esteemed historians produce a valuable reference book on World War II. Easy to use, the book is helpful in understanding the war's background.

Frank Sanello, *Spielberg.* Dallas, TX: Taylor, 1996. Sanello's sound biography of the famed director includes a decent chapter on the making of *Schindler's List.*

Emilie Schindler, with Erika Rosenberg, *Where Light and Shadow Meet: A Memoir.* New York: W.W. Norton, 1996. Oskar Schindler's wife has left an important document that helps explain the complex Oskar Schindler. Her role in helping Jews survive the war is more fully explained than in any previous book, and the reader can still feel the love she has for her husband, despite his unfaithfulness.

William L. Shirer, *The Rise and Fall of the Third Reich.* New York: Simon and Schuster, 1960. Still one of the best sources of information on Germany under Nazi rule.

Eric Silver, *The Book of the Just: The Unsung Heroes Who Rescued Jews from Hitler*. New York: Grove Press, 1992. Silver profiles different individuals who rescued Jews during World War II, including Schindler. Silver's oral history account is very useful in understanding why people acted so courageously, and in reminding readers that other, less famous "Schindlers" also risked their lives to help others.

John Toland, *Adolf Hitler*. Garden City, NY: Doubleday, 1976. A readable, complete biography of the German leader.

Periodicals

Luitgard N. Wundheiler, "Oskar Schindler's Moral Development During the Holocaust," *Humboldt Journal of Social Social Relation*, Fall/Winter and Spring/Summer 1985–1986. Wundheiler explores Oskar Schindler's moral progression as the war years unfolded and attempts to explain what made Schindler embark on his rescue efforts.

Television Programs

A&E Biography, "Oskar Schindler: The Man Behind the List," 1998. This episode of the long-running television series surveys the life and times of Oskar Schindler.

Thames Television Productions, "Schindler," 1983. Though not as comprehensive as the A&E documentary, this program contains some illuminating quotes from associates of Schindler and from some of the people he saved.

Index

Picture Credits

About the Author

John F. Wukovits is a junior high school teacher and writer from Trenton, Michigan, who specializes in history and biography. Besides biographies of Anne Frank, Jim Carrey, Stephen King, and Martin Luther King Jr. for Lucent, he has written biographies of the World War II commander Admiral Clifton Sprague, Barry Sanders, Tim Allen, Jack Nicklaus, Vince Lombardi, and Wyatt Earp. A graduate of the University of Notre Dame, Wukovits is the father of three daughters—Amy, Julie, and Karen.